Evaluating What Good Teachers Do

Eight Research-Based Standards for Assessing Teacher Excellence

James H. Stronge

EYE ON EDUCATION
6 DEPOT WAY WEST, SUITE 106
LARCHMONT, NY 10538
(914) 833–0551
(914) 833–0761 fax
www.eyeoneducation.com

A sincere effort has been made to supply the identity of those who have created specific strategies. Any omissions have been unintentional.

Copyright © 2010 Eye On Education, Inc. All Rights Reserved.

For information about permission to reproduce selections from this book, write: Eye On Education, Permissions Dept., Suite 106, 6 Depot Way West, Larchmont, NY 10538.

Library of Congress Cataloging-in-Publication Data

Stronge, James H.

 Evaluating what good teachers do : eight research-based standards for assessing teacher excellence / James H. Stronge.

 p. cm.

 ISBN 978-1-59667-157-7

 1. Effective teaching—Case studies. 2. Educational innovations—Case studies. 3. School improvement programs—Case studies. 4. Learning, Psychology of—Case studies. I. Title.

 LB1025.3.S7887 2010

 371.14′4—dc22

2010009763

10 9 8 7 6 5 4 3 2 1

The James H. Stronge Research-to-Practice Series

Evaluating What Good Teachers Do:
Eight Research-Based Standards for Assessing Teacher Excellence
James H. Stronge

Effective Teachers = Student Achievement:
What the Research Says
James H. Stronge

Student Achievement Goal Setting:
Using Data to Improve Teaching and Learning
James H. Stronge and Leslie W. Grant

The Supportive Learning Environment:
Effective Teaching Practices
Jennifer L. Hindman, James H. Stronge, and Leslie W. Grant

Planning, Instruction, and Assessment:
Effective Teaching Practices
Leslie W. Grant, Jennifer L. Hindman, and James H. Stronge

Also Available from These Authors

Handbook on Teacher Evaluation:
Assessing and Improving Performance
James H. Stronge and Pamela D. Tucker

Handbook on Educational Specialist Evaluation:
Assessing and Improving Performance
James H. Stronge and Pamela D. Tucker

Handbook on Teacher Portfolios for Evaluation
and Professional Development
Pamela Tucker, James Stronge, and Christopher Gareis

Other Great Titles from Eye On Education

Leading School Change: 9 Strategies to Bring Everybody On Board
Todd Whitaker

Classroom Walkthroughs to Improve Teaching and Learning
Donald S. Kachur, Judith A. Stout, and Claudia L. Edwards

Help Teachers Engage Students: Action Tools for Administrators
Annette Brinkman, Gary Forlini, and Ellen Williams

Acknowledgments

As with all writing projects that I have undertaken, *Evaluating What Good Teachers Do: Eight Research-Based Standards for Assessing Teacher Excellence*, is a work whose development relied on the capable and generous contributions of numerous colleagues and friends. I would like to express my appreciation to them.

My colleagues and graduate students from the College of William and Mary offered invaluable support for this project. In particular, I would to express my appreciation to Xianxuan Xu. Xian currently is a Ph.D. candidate in the College of William and Mary's Educational Policy, Planning, and Leadership Program and my graduate assistant. She contributed to the book through her capable assistance with the background review of the extant research presented in the chapters and her careful editing of the manuscript. Xian is a highly able young educator who promises to make significant contributions to the field of education. She aspires to return to her native China as a university professor following the completion of her doctoral work, and I am convinced that she will be most successful in her academic career.

I have enjoyed the opportunity over the past twenty-plus years of consulting in many school districts and other educational organizations in designing, piloting, and training educators to use teacher performance evaluation systems. Based on this work, many administrators and teachers from these varied school districts assisted with field-testing teacher evaluation systems based on the performance standards, data collection tools, and performance appraisal rubrics incorporated in the book. I would like to acknowledge the contributions and express my appreciation to the very capable educators associated with these varied school districts. In particular, regional education agencies and school districts in Florida, Pennsylvania, and Virginia have played prominent roles in refining my work on teacher performance evaluation systems. An excellent example of the type of comprehensive teacher evaluation system that is explored in the book is that used by the Greenville County, South Carolina, Public Schools.*

Finally, I wish to acknowledge, you, the readers, who have embraced other books that I have written. In some small way I hope this new book, *Evaluating What Good Teachers Do: Eight Research-Based Standards for Assessing Teacher Excellence*, might enhance the important work you do. Thank you.

---

* To avoid neglecting anyone, I chose not to attempt to identify all school districts and regional/state educational agencies with which I have collaborated in designing and implementing teacher and administrator performance evaluation systems. Nonetheless, to each, please know that I sincerely appreciate the valued contributions you have made to my education and that I most assuredly value your continued friendship.

About the Author

James H. Stronge is the Heritage Professor in the Educational Policy, Planning, and Leadership Area at the College of William and Mary, Williamsburg, Virginia. His research interests include policy and practice related to teacher quality, and teacher and administrator evaluation. His work on teacher quality focuses on how to identify effective teachers and how to enhance teacher effectiveness. Dr. Stronge has presented his research at state, national, and international conferences such as the American Educational Research Association, American Association of School Administrators, Asia-Pacific Conference on Gifted, Association for Supervision and Curriculum Development, European Council of International Schools. National Evaluation Institute, and University Council for Educational Administration. Additionally, he has worked extensively with local school districts and other educational organizations on issues related to teacher effectiveness, teacher selection, and teacher and administrator evaluation.

Dr. Stronge has authored, coauthored, or edited twenty-two books and more than 100 articles, chapters, and technical reports. Selected books have been translated and published in Arabic, Mandarin, Italian, Korean, Portuguese, and Vietnamese. Some of his recent books include:

- *Student Achievement Goal Setting: Using Data to Improve Teaching and Learning* (Eye On Education, 2009)

- *Qualities of Effective Principals* (Association for Supervision and Curriculum Development, 2008)

- *Qualities of Effective Teaching,* 2nd Ed. (Association for Supervision and Curriculum Development, 2007)

- *The Teacher Quality Index: A Protocol for Teacher Selection* (Association for Supervision and Curriculum Development, 2006)

- *Teacher Pay and Teacher Quality: Attracting, Developing, and Retaining the Best Teachers* (Corwin Press, 2006)

- *Linking Teacher Evaluation and Student Achievement* (Association for Supervision and Curriculum Development, 2005)

- *Evaluating Teaching,* 2nd Ed. (Corwin Press, 2005)

Dr. Stronge has been a teacher, counselor, and district-level administrator. His doctorate is in the area of Educational Administration and Planning from the University of Alabama. He may be contacted at: The College of William and Mary, School of Education, P.O. Box 8795, Williamsburg, VA 23187–8795; 757-221-2339; or http://wmpeople.wm.edu/jhstro.

Contents

Preface

So why bother with evaluating teacher effectiveness? Because teachers matter inordinately to student learning. As I have written in other places, *teacher effectiveness = student success.* "Without capable, high quality teachers in America's classrooms, no educational reform effort can possibly succeed" (Stronge & Tucker, 2003a, p. 3). Moreover, "without high quality evaluation systems, we cannot know if we have high quality teachers" (p. 3).

In an editorial in *Education Week*, Hiebert, Gallimore, and Stigler (2003) expressed a sentiment that I fully endorse:

> To improve teaching, many say, the profession must find better teachers. Celebrity teachers, such as Jaime Escalante, are held up as models of what's possible and are hailed as heroes of the profession. The trouble is that most students do not have Jaime Escalante as a teacher, and more Escalantes are hard to find.
>
> Identifying a few excellent teachers and hoping others will copy their methods has not improved teaching in the average American classroom. Teaching, as most students experience it, has not changed for decades. Why? Because the average classroom is not affected much by what the few celebrity teachers do. To make a dent in the learning experiences for most students, educators must find a way to improve the quality of instruction in the average classroom. Even slight improvements in the average classroom, accumulated over time, would have a more profound effect on students around the country than recruiting a hundred more Escalantes into the classroom. (p. 1)

The primary purpose of *Evaluating What Good Teachers Do: Eight Research-Based Standards for Assessing Teacher Effectiveness* is to help both teachers and their evaluators collect more comprehensive and accurate assessment data for judging teacher effectiveness. The only way I know that schools can improve student achievement is to improve teacher effectiveness. If we can succeed in recruiting, supporting, assessing, and keeping capable teachers, we will go a great distance in improving our schools and, in turn, substantially embellishing the learning opportunities of students.

Part I

Performance Standards
for Teachers

1

How to Assess Teacher Quality

School reform doesn't happen in Washington, Ottawa, London, or, for that matter, any other capital. It doesn't occur at the school board level or even at the school, for the most part. *Evaluating What Good Teachers Do: Eight Research-Based Standards for Assessing Teacher Excellence* is built on the foundation that the classroom—not the school—is the place on which we must focus for improved student performance. When one teacher improves her or his capacity to help students learn, then, and only then, does school improvement occur. And the reason is quite simple: *teacher success = student success*.

Evaluating What Good Teachers Do: Eight Research-Based Standards for Assessing Teacher Excellence focuses on providing a research-based framework for teacher assessment. This introductory chapter provides the foundation for defining, designing, and applying teacher performance standards. Specifically, this chapter addresses the following foundational issues:

♦ What are teacher performance standards and how are they used?

♦ What are quality indicators and how are they used?

♦ How can teacher performance standards be documented?

♦ How can teacher performance standards be rated?

♦ Why are performance standards important for ensuring teacher quality?

What Are Teacher Performance Standards and How Are They Used?

Importance of Defining the Job of the Teacher

Tēach'ēr, n. 1. One who teaches or instructs.[1]

Although it is common practice to develop job descriptions for an array of educational positions, interestingly, the job of the teacher often is neglected. Perhaps because we believe that we so readily understand what it means to be a teacher, or perhaps because it is such a complex and encompassing job, we just don't go to the trouble of providing an operational definition. Yet, without a clear, objective, and accurate description of the required job responsibilities, it isn't feasible to provide an effective evaluation of performance. If *actual* performance is to be compared with *expected* performance, then there must be an alignment between job requirements and job evaluation. In fact, the foundation of a quality teacher evaluation system is the use of clearly described and well-documented job performance standards for all educators—in other words, the job responsibilities.

Overview of Performance Standards[2]

For teacher performance evaluation to be fair and comprehensive, it is necessary to describe the performance standards of teachers with sufficient detail and accuracy so that both teachers and their supervisors can reasonably understand the job expectations. In essence, a set of performance standards is a detailed job description.

The expectations for teacher performance are defined using a two-tiered approach (Figure 1.1).

Figure 1.1. Model for Teacher Performance Standards and Quality Indicators

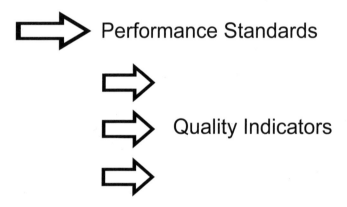

Source: Adapted from J.H. Stronge's *Goals and Roles Evaluation Model.* It is used here with permission from the author.

Performance standards are the major units (i.e., major job responsibilities) of the teacher's job, whereas quality indicators are the specific, observable, measurable aspects of these major job responsibilities. Performance standards and quality indicators will be explained, in turn.

Suggested Teacher Performance Standards

Performance standards are the job responsibilities or duties performed by a teacher. Consequently, the performance standards represent the major job responsibilities that a teacher fulfills. The performance standards form the basis for the development of job descriptions and, thus, should also form the basis for a job evaluation. Additionally, the teacher performance standards are intended to provide specification of role expectations. In other words, they provide clarity on the precise nature of the key aspects of the teacher's job. Figure 1.2 is a set of suggested teacher performance standards.

Figure 1.2. Suggested Teacher Performance Standards

Suggested Teacher Performance Standards

1. Professional Knowledge

   The teacher demonstrates an understanding of the curriculum, subject content, and the developmental needs of students by providing relevant learning experiences.

2. Data-Driven Planning

   The teacher's planning uses appropriate curricula, instructional strategies, and resources to address the needs of all students.

3. Instructional Delivery

   The teacher promotes student learning by addressing individual learning differences and by using effective instructional strategies.

4. Assessment of Learning

   The teacher systematically gathers, analyzes, and uses data to measure student progress, guide instruction, and provide timely feedback.

5. Learning Environment

   The teacher provides a well-managed, safe, student-centered environment that is academically challenging and respectful.

6. Communication and Advocacy

   The teacher communicates effectively with students, school personnel, families, and the community.

7. Professionalism

   The teacher maintains a professional demeanor, participates in professional growth opportunities, and contributes to the profession.

8. Student Progress

   The work of the teacher results in acceptable, measurable progress based on established standards.

Alignment of Teacher Performance Standards with Qualities of Effective Teachers

The eight teacher performance standards described in Figure 1.2 form the foundation for the teacher performance assessment system detailed throughout *Evaluating What Good Teachers Do*. In fact, until the key work of the teacher—the teacher performance standards—are understood and agreed upon, all other aspects of a comprehensive evaluation system are superfluous. We observe and collect other relevant evidence, not in the abstract, but based on a given set of performance expectations—the performance standards. Furthermore, we evaluate based on how well a teacher's performance matches the prescribed work; again, the performance standards.

If the selection of a teacher's performance standards is so fundamentally important to the overall assessment of the teacher's work, then it is incumbent that these standards have a solid grounding in the research of what makes teachers effective.

Chapters 2 through 9 explore the research base upon which each of the eight respective teacher performance standards is grounded.

What Are Quality Indicators and How Are They Used?

Overview of Quality Indicators

The assumption upon which a system of teacher performance standards is built is that teachers—regardless of what their particular assignments might be—are far more alike than they are different. Nonetheless, although the use of a common set of instructional performance standards tends to work very well for most teachers, preK-12, the actual work of a high school teacher, for example, a chemistry teacher, differs markedly from that of a fourth grade teacher. Likewise, the role of a chemistry teacher is different from those of other high school teachers, for example, a Spanish teacher or a biology teacher. Practically speaking, however, it would be virtually impossible to create and implement a teacher evaluation system with separate sets of performance standards for every grade level, subject matter, or other job distinctions that exist in a school or school system. Yet, if we don't account for important differences in teacher roles and responsibilities, the evaluation process becomes far too generic and, thus, completely irrelevant. So how do we adjust for these important differences in teacher work? It is through the customization of the quality indicators—the second level used in defining and describing the work of the teacher (see the visual provided in Figure 1.1, page 4).

Although performance standards describe the essence of the job, a more specific unit of performance—quality indicators—is needed for actual documentation of the accomplishments of the teacher. Performance standards constitute the basic units of the job, as described above. However, performance standards do not lend themselves readily to direct classroom observation or other types of documentation or measurement.

How Quality Indicators Are Used

Quality indicators are used in the teacher evaluation system to do just what the term implies: *indicate* in observable behaviors, the types and quality of performance associated with performance standards. Thus, a quality indicator is a tangible behavior that can be observed or documented to determine the degree to which a teacher is fulfilling a given performance standard.

Evaluators and teachers are encouraged to review the lists of quality indicators provided in the book, and to customize them—supplementing, modifying, or reducing as appropriate—for a particular teacher work assignment or situation. Figure 1.3 illustrates quality indicators for the *Student Progress* performance standard.

Figure 1.3. Sample Set of Teacher Quality Indicators

Performance Standard 8: Student Progress

The work of the teacher results in acceptable, measurable progress based on established performance expectations.

Sample Quality Indicators

The teacher

♦ sets measurable and appropriate achievement goals for student progress.

♦ gathers and analyzes data on student academic achievement through standardized test results and other student performance sources.

♦ uses formative assessment to regularly monitor student progress and modify instruction as needed.

♦ provides evidence that achievement goals have been met.

♦ communicates/collaborates with colleagues in order to improve students' performance.

Quality indicators are provided to help teachers and their evaluators clarify and document performance standards (i.e., job responsibilities). All quality indicators, however, may not be applicable for a particular teaching assignment. In fact, some teaching positions may need to identify specialized quality indicators. Special education teachers, for example, are required to participate in individualized education program (IEP) meetings and maintain appropriate documentation regarding student performance. Another example is that science teachers may need to add a quality indicator regarding lab safety for *Standard 5: Learning Environment*.

It is important to note that quality indicators are merely *examples* of behaviors. Although sample lists of quality indicators are provided for each teacher standard throughout the book, these lists of quality indicators are not intended to be exhaustive. Rather, they are merely *examples* of typical behaviors that may serve as evidence that a teacher meets the given standard. Additionally, any set of quality indicators should have the features described in Figure 1.4 on page 8.

Figure 1.4. Features of Well-Designed Teacher Quality Indicators

Key Features of Quality Indicators

♦ Be observable or measurable as an indicator of whether the given performance standard—for instance, *Professional Knowledge*—is being performed.

♦ Should not be considered as an exhaustive set of all possible observable behaviors for the associated performance standard, but rather as a representative set of behaviors.

♦ Be modifiable and customizable to fit the particular job requirements of the teachers being evaluated (i.e., chemistry teachers, third grade teachers).

♦ Serve the purpose of documenting the performance standard, but not be the level at which performance ratings are applied. (The performance standard—not the quality indicator—should be the unit of analysis and the level at which a performance rating is given.)

♦ Should not be used as a checklist in which all quality indicators must be checked-off in order for a teacher to receive an acceptable rating on the given performance standard.

Figure 1.5 illustrates the relationship between performance standards and quality indicators, wherein the quality indicators are subsumed under the guiding performance standard.

Figure 1.5. Relationship between Performance Standards and Quality Indicators

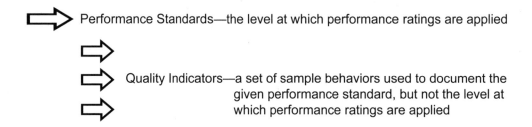

Performance Standards—the level at which performance ratings are applied

Quality Indicators—a set of sample behaviors used to document the given performance standard, but not the level at which performance ratings are applied

In summary, a list of quality indicators is *not* exhaustive, and is not intended to be prescriptive. Teachers may not be expected to demonstrate each quality indicator; rather, they are expected to demonstrate overall performance within *all* performance standards. Additionally, performance ratings will *not* be made at the quality indicator level, but at the performance standard level instead.

How Can Teacher Performance Standards Be Documented?

Documenting Teacher Performance Standards

The role of a teacher requires a performance assessment system that acknowledges the complexities of the job. Given the complexity of teacher's work, attempting to document the work with one method or data source simple isn't sensible or feasible. Instead, using multiple data sources can provide for a comprehensive and authentic "performance portrait" of the teacher's work. The multiple sources of information described in Figure 1.6 (page 10) can be used to provide comprehensive and accurate feedback on teacher performance.

Observation

Direct classroom observation can be a useful way to collect information on teacher performance; as a standalone data-collection process, however, it has major limitations. If the purpose of a teacher evaluation system is to provide a comprehensive picture of performance in order to guide professional growth, then classroom observations should be only one piece of the data-collection puzzle. Furthermore, observations can take on a variety of forms and can be conducted in a variety of settings—ranging from quick, drop-by classroom visits to formal, preplanned observational reviews.[3] Types of observations might include formal, informal, and walkthrough, among others.

Formal Observations

In *formal observations*, the evaluator conducts a structured or semistructured, planned observation—either announced or unannounced—typically of a teacher who is presenting a lesson to or interacting with students. Evaluators can use formal observations as one source of information to determine whether a teacher is meeting expectations for performance standards. Typically, the evaluator provides feedback about the observation during a review conference with the teacher. Formal classroom observations should last a specified period of time—for example, thirty or forty-five minutes, or the duration of full lesson. For maximum value, the building level administrator should ensure that formal observations occur throughout the year.

Informal Observations

Informal observations are intended to provide more frequent information on a wide variety of contributions made by teachers in the classroom or to the school community as a whole. Evaluators are encouraged to conduct informal observations by observing instruction and noninstructional routines at various times throughout the evaluation cycle.* These informal observations typically are less structured than formal observations.

---

* An evaluation cycle refers to an ongoing process of data collection, evaluator–evaluatee discussion, summative review, and performance improvement. The various cyclical steps in a quality evaluation system (e.g., classroom observation—feedback—improvement) are inextricably linked and seamless.

Figure 1.6. Recommended Data Sources for a Comprehensive Teacher Evaluation System

Data Source	Definition
Observations	Observations, including formal and informal observations, are intended to provide direct, naturalistic information on the work of a teacher, student behaviors, and the dynamic interaction between teacher and learners. In addition to classroom observations, observations can be conducted in a variety of job-relevant settings (e.g., a conference with a parent, a committee meeting, a presentation to the school staff). Observations are an important source of teacher performance information, but should *never* be used as a sole source for documenting evaluation performance.
Portfolio/Data Log	A portfolio or data log includes artifacts that provide documentation for the teacher performance standards. The portfolio/data log should emphasize naturally occurring artifacts from teachers' work (i.e., lesson plans, instructional units, student assessments).
Student Surveys	Student surveys provide information to the teacher about students' perceptions of how the teacher is performing. Surveys—a key aspect of the 360-degree approach to evaluation—have been used extensively in business and government settings, and to a lesser extent in education. There is ample evidence, however, to support the use of client surveys in teacher evaluation.
Student Achievement/ Performance Goal Setting	Teachers have a definite impact on student learning and academic performance. Depending on grade level, content area, and ability level, appropriate measures of student performance should be identified to provide information on the learning gains of students. Value-Added Methods (VAM) performance measures include available standardized test results as well as other pertinent data. With proper use, teachers can set goals for improving student achievement based on appropriate performance measures. Thus, VAM can be an important component for teacher evaluation. However, student achievement, alone, should *never* be used as the sole source for evaluating teacher performance.

Note: Although all of the above data sources can play a prominent role in documenting teacher performance, observation and portfolios/data logs are featured in this book. For detailed information on options for including student achievement Value-Added Methods (VAM), how to develop and use student achievement goal setting, how to select and use student surveys, and other related teacher evaluation topics, see *Want to Know More Suggested Books Related to Teacher Effectiveness and Teacher Evaluation* in Part II of this book.

Informal observations might include observing instruction for a short duration (say, ten to fifteen minutes) or observing work in nonclassroom settings at various times throughout the school year. For example, an informal observation might include briefly visiting a classroom during a science lab experiment or observing a teacher participating in a faculty meeting or committee meeting. An important factor for evaluators to remember when collecting informal observation data is to focus on specific, factual descriptions of performance. Also, it is important to obtain a representative sampling of performance observations through regular, repeat visits to classrooms.[4]

Walkthrough Observations

Walkthrough observations have been popularized in recent years as a means for documenting and assessing practices and trends throughout a school.[5] Typically, walkthrough observations are designed to provide brief (three- to five-minute) visits in multiple classrooms. Although walkthrough visits can be helpful in checking for standard instructional practices or for vertical and horizontal curriculum articulation across the school, be cautious in relying on these visits for individual teacher evaluation. Visits of three to five minutes—even if conducted frequently—simply do not do justice to teachers in terms of understanding their instructional or assessment practices, student time-on-task, learning environment, and so forth.

Portfolios/Data Logs

Portfolios—or *data logs*—are an important part of a comprehensive approach for documenting teacher performance. Generally, a teacher evaluation portfolio is considered to be "a structured collection of selected artifacts that demonstrate a teacher's competence and growth."[6] A data log as part of a teacher evaluation data collection system typically is considered to be a more succinct collection of artifacts.[7] Both portfolios and data logs are designed to serve as a compliment to teacher observation in order to provide a fuller, fairer, more comprehensive view of teacher performance. Throughout the chapters that follow, a discussion of portfolios and data logs is presented collectively, as most of the procedures and many of the artifacts for both are interchangeable.

In systems such as the Greenville County, South Carolina, Schools, the teacher evaluation portfolio serves as a system for collecting data and documenting work quality during each evaluation cycle. Specifically, the portfolio houses pertinent data that confirm that the teacher meets the established performance standards. Written analysis and reflection about artifacts should be included in the portfolio to provide insight into the rationale for the events and process documented in each entry. In a system such as this, the portfolio becomes an official document that is maintained by the teacher and reviewed periodically by the evaluator. The amount of material that can be collected is limited to the size of the binder provided by the school district; thus, the teacher must be selective regarding what artifacts to include. Additionally, the portfolio or data log should only include material that is applicable for the individual teacher's evaluation cycle and directly related to the teacher performance standards.

Evaluation portfolios or data logs, in general, should provide a collection of written records and documents produced by the teacher as a part of the teacher's regular job responsibilities. Consequently, artifacts to be included in a portfolio or data log should rarely be developed just for the portfolio/data log; rather, they should be naturally occurring documents. For example, artifacts for a special education teacher might include copies of IEPs developed, lesson plans related to those IEPs, syllabi developed or adapted for a given class, and representative samples of student work. Additional artifacts that are likely to be available and meaningful as part of a data collection process that is designed to accurately reflect the teacher's job performance could include the following examples:

- Lesson plans,
- Instructional materials,
- Student assessments,
- Forms developed and/or used for record keeping,
- Significant correspondence and memos,
- Schedules, logs, or calendars of activities, and
- Evidence of professional development activities.

Using Multiple Data Sources

Some teacher standards are better documented through classroom observation (e.g., teaching style or classroom management) whereas other standards may require additional documentation. For example, *Standard 2: Data-driven Planning* may necessitate review of the teacher's lesson plans and *Standard 4: Assessment of Learning* may necessitate review of the teacher's student assessments. Such evidence often is collected by the teacher and presented as a portfolio or data log as a complement to the supervisor-conducted observations. Figure 1.7 offers a matrix connecting portfolios/data logs and observation with the eight featured teacher performance standards.

How Can Teacher Performance Standards Be Rated?

Rating Scales

Connecting the performance standard to the data sources and, then, to the applicable rating scale can be described with the following three questions:

Question 1: *What is expected* of the teacher? (The performance standard.)

Question 2: *How will we know* if the teacher is fulfilling the performance standard? (The data sources.)

Question 3: *How well* is the teacher fulfilling the performance standard? (The rating scale.)

It is Question 3—the *how well*—that is addressed by applying a rating scale and the related performance appraisal rubric to the given performance standard.

**Figure 1.7. Aligning Selected Data Sources
with Teacher Performance Standards**

Performance Standard	Observation	Portfolio/Data Log	Other Data Sources
1. Professional Knowledge	P	P	TBD
2. Data-Driven Planning	S	P	TBD
3. Instructional Delivery	P	S	TBD
4. Assessment of Learning	S	P	TBD
5. Learning Environment	P	S	TBD
6. Communication and Advocacy	S	P	TBD
7. Professionalism	S	P	TBD
8. Student Progress	S	P	P

Note: P = primary data source; S = secondary data source; TBD = to be determined.

The rating scale provides a description of levels of how well the teacher performance standards (i.e., job responsibilities) are performed on a continuum from, say, "exemplary" to "unsatisfactory." The rating is applied in most instances only in a summative (cumulative, end-of-evaluation-cycle) evaluation, but not in formative (ongoing, throughout-the-evaluation-cycle) settings.

The use of a rating scale enables evaluators to acknowledge effective performance (i.e., "exemplary" and "proficient") and provides one or more levels of feedback for teachers not meeting expectations (i.e., "needs improvement" and "unsatisfactory"). Rating scales for teachers in various school districts typically range from a two-point scale (i.e., Satisfactory–Unsatisfactory, Pass–Fail) to four- or five-point scales (i.e., Exemplary–Unsatisfactory, Exceeds Standard–Does Not Meet Standard).

Regardless of what type of rating scale is used, an inherent problem in their use exists: Rating scales can be too subjective. To illustrate, if Evaluator A views a given aspect of a teacher's performance and rates it as "Exceeds Standard" and Evaluator B views the same performance and rates it "Needs Improvement," then there is no trustworthiness in the ratings. Rating scales should not perpetuate highly subjective reviews of a teachers' performance; this speculative process is simply unjust. Rather, rating scales should improve trustworthiness of evaluators' ratings through interrater agreement (reliability) based on documented evidence for established performance standards. Despite the problems inherent in rating scales, the absence of them can be even more problematic. Therefore, it is recommended that a rating scale be used, applied systematically, and be based on the best possible performance evidence available. In using performance rating scales, consider the following two points:

◆ Determining the quality of performance is more than examining a set of facts; it requires consideration of the context of the work, results, and so forth. Thus, evaluation, ultimately, *is* about judgment, albeit judgment based squarely on performance.

◆ The absence of a rating scale can be problematic. Consider, for example, the possibility of replacing a rating scale with totally narrative feedback. Indeed, narrative comments are valuable to highlight performance and to illuminate specific behaviors, recommendations, and so forth. Nonetheless, it would be extraordinarily difficult to achieve any reasonable measure of interrater reliability among evaluators and across multiple evaluatees based on these narrative comments.[8]

Throughout *Part I: Performance Standards for Teachers*, three-, four-, and five-point rating scales are used to illustrate how to apply a rating scale to teacher performance standard. To illustrate, the definitions in Figure 1.8 offer general descriptions for a four-point rating system.

Figure 1.8. Suggested Definitions of Terms in Rating Scale

Rating	Definition
Exemplary	High-quality performance: ◆ Exceeds the requirements contained in the job description as expressed in the evaluation criteria ◆ Continually seeks opportunities to learn and apply new skills. ◆ Consistently exhibits behaviors that have a strong positive impact on students and the school climate and serves as a role model to others.
Proficient	High-quality performance: ◆ Meets the requirements contained in the job description as expressed in the evaluation criteria. ◆ Demonstrates willingness to learn and apply new skills. ◆ Exhibits behaviors that have a positive impact on students and school climate.
Developing/ Needs Improvement	Inconsistent performance: ◆ Results in less-than-quality-work performance and student behavior. ◆ Leads to areas for professional improvement being jointly identified and planned between the teacher and supervisor. ◆ Will result in an *unsatisfactory* rating if it continues.
Unsatisfactory	Poor-quality performance: ◆ Does not meet the requirements contained in the job description as expressed in the evaluation criteria. ◆ May result in the employee may not being recommended for continued employment, if a plan of improvement is not met.

Note: Ratings are applied to performance standards, but not to quality indicators.

Performance Appraisal Rubric

Even when rating scales are well-defined, it isn't enough to ensure consistency (reliability) in judging the quality of teacher work. Thus, a second tool—a *performance appraisal rubric*—is provided for each of the eight identified teacher standards. The performance appraisal rubric describes acceptable performance levels for each teacher performance standard. It relates the measure of performance expected of teachers for each standard and provides a general description of what a rating entails. Thus, the performance appraisal rubric can be used as a type of discrepancy analysis:

Expected Performance Compared to Actual Performance = Performance Rating

The performance appraisal rubrics guide evaluators in assessing *how well* a standard is performed, and they are provided to increase reliability among evaluators. By using performance appraisal rubrics, there is the opportunity to generate defensibility for ratings, greater reliability among evaluators, and enhanced fairness to teachers as evaluatees. Figure 1.9 is an example of four-point performance appraisal rubric. Part II of the book offers a comprehensive set of three-, four-, and five-point performance appraisal rubric options.

Figure 1.9. Example of a Performance Appraisal Rubric

Standard 8: Student Performance

Exemplary *In addition to meeting the standard...*	Proficient*	Developing/ Needs Improvement	Unsatisfactory
The teacher attains a high level of student achievement with all populations of learners.	The work of the teacher results in acceptable, measurable progress based on established standards.	The work of the teacher results in student growth but does not meet the established standard and/or is not achieved with all populations taught by the teacher.	The work of the teacher does not achieve acceptable student growth.

* "Proficient" is the baseline of acceptable performance for teachers and is the actual performance standard.

Performance appraisal rubrics are not behavioral objectives (e.g., "four times out of five"). Rather, they are designed to:

♦ Generally delineate the type and quality of performance within each rating;

♦ Require that ratings be based on the documented evidence; and

◆ Restrict the scope of judgment that can be used in determining a given rating.

Even with performance appraisal rubrics, rating a teacher's performance is not a fine science—there still will be differences in judgment. However, with the use of the rubrics, these differences can be substantially reduced, resulting in increased interrater agreement. A few guidelines that further enhance the value and defensibility of ratings based on performance appraisal rubrics include the following:

◆ When comparing the documented evidence with the performance rubric, start with the "Meets Standard" or "Proficient" rating and move up or down the scale only when the evidence justifies it.

◆ When all of the collected evidence doesn't fit within a single rating rubric (which typically is the case), select the rating where the *preponderance of evidence* lies.

◆ Provide teachers with the full set of performance appraisal rubrics so that they have full disclosure of the level of performance that is expected and a fair opportunity to meet those expectations.

◆ Consistently train evaluators in the use of the performance appraisal rubrics, with special attention given to practicing the rubrics in simulated settings.

Why Are Performance Standards Important for Ensuring Teacher Quality?

Using teacher performance standards to evaluate teacher effectiveness is first, about documenting the quality of teacher work; then, the focus shifts to helping teachers improve their performance and to holding them accountable for their work. Given the emphasis on teacher effectiveness as expressed in federal and state legislation, public policy, and practice in every state (and, for that matter, many nations throughout the world), a premium must be placed on high-quality teacher evaluation systems to a degree that didn't heretofore exist.

The primary purposes of any worthy teacher evaluation system include the following:

◆ Contribute to the successful achievement of the goals and objectives defined in the educational plan for the school or school system;

◆ Provide a basis for instructional improvement through productive teacher appraisal and professional growth;

◆ Improve the quality of instruction and other key job responsibilities by assuring accountability for teacher performance; and

◆ Share responsibility for evaluation between the teacher and the evaluator in a collaborative process that promotes self-growth, instructional effectiveness, and improvement of overall job performance.

So why does it matter that we have clear and consistent teacher performance standards? Because regardless of how well a program is designed, it is only as effective as the people who implement it.[9] "Thus, a conceptually sound, well-designed, and properly implemented evaluation system for teachers is an important—indeed, essential—component of an effective school."[10] The following chapters and sections of have as their fundamental focus identifying, documenting, and consistently applying teacher performance standards as we seek to improve and support quality teaching in our schools.

Notes

1 McKechnie, J. L. (1983). p. 1871.

2 Portions of the following section are adapted from Tucker, P. D., & Stronge, J. H. (2003b).

3 Stronge, J. H., & Tucker, P. D. (2003b).

4 Stronge, J. H., & Tucker, P. D. (2003b).

5 Downey, C. J., Steffy, B. E., English, F. W., Frase, L. E., & Poston, W. K., Jr. (2004).

6 Tucker, P. D., Stronge, J. H., & Gareis, C. R. (2002). p. 3.

7 Wolf, K., Lichtenstein, G., & Stevenson, C. (1997).

8 Stronge, J. H., & Tucker, P. D. (2003b).

9 Stronge, J. H. (2006).

10 Stronge, J. H. (2006). p. 2.

2

Professional Knowledge[*]

In its most fundamental definition, *to teach* means to impart knowledge and skills. Equally fundamental to the understanding of teaching, one cannot impart knowledge unless one possesses knowledge. Although knowledge, alone, will not suffice to make someone an effective teacher, it certainly is a basic building block to teaching. Thus, possessing the requisite professional knowledge is an essential ingredient to becoming a good teacher. This chapter, the first to explore in-depth the eight recommended teacher performance standards, focuses on the professional knowledge of the teacher. The framework that is used here and in subsequent chapters addresses five key questions related to the *Professional Knowledge* performance standard for teachers:

♦ What does *professional knowledge* mean?

♦ What does the research say about *professional knowledge* of the teacher?

♦ What are research-based quality indicators for *professional knowledge*?

♦ How can *professional knowledge* be documented?

♦ What are rating scale options for *professional knowledge*?

What Does *Professional Knowledge* Mean?

Professional knowledge certainly encompasses knowledge of subject matter. A teacher's understanding of subject facts, concepts, principles, and the methods through which they are integrated cognitively determine the teacher's pedagogical thinking and decision making. The research on this issue consistently has suggested that strong content knowledge is positively associated with students' learning, particularly in mathematics at all grade levels.[1] In essence, one cannot teach math unless one knows math (the same applies for any other subject matter). However, the professional knowledge that is essential to be an effective teacher extends well beyond knowledge of subject matter to encompass at least the factors identified in Figure 2.1.

---

[*] A standard format and common language are used throughout Chapters 2 to 9 so as to provide comparability and ease-of-use for the eight teacher performance standards presented in the chapters. Consequently, there is purposeful overlap in introductory language used in the chapters. The intent is that this selective use of repetitive language will serve to reinforce the concepts and practices discussed throughout the book.

**Figure 2.1. Key Areas of Professional
Knowledge for Effective Teachers**

Knowledge Area	Focus
Subject-matter knowledge	Content to teach
Pedagogical knowledge*	How to teach
Curricular knowledge	What to teach
Learner knowledge	Who to teach
Cultural/community knowledge	Sensitivity to who and where one teaches

Note: For purposes of evaluating teacher effectiveness, pedagogical knowledge is included more typically in the *Instructional Delivery* performance standard rather than *Professional Knowledge* standard.

This simple framework provides a starting point to understanding the multifaceted dimensions of the knowledge required to teach effectively. Teaching is not merely stand-and-deliver; rather, it is a far more complex undertaking. Just anyone cannot walk in off the street and start teaching. A specialized body of knowledge is a hallmark of any true profession and, indeed, teaching can lay claim to a specialized, complex, intricate, and constantly changing and renewing body of knowledge.

Figure 2.2 provides two sample definitions for *professional knowledge*. These definitions can be used to help operationalize the teacher performance standard, *Professional Knowledge*.

Figure 2.2. Sample Definitions for the *Professional Knowledge* **Performance Standard**

Sample 1. Professional Knowledge

The teacher demonstrates an understanding of the curriculum, subject content, and the developmental needs of students by providing relevant learning experiences.

Sample 2. Professional Knowledge/Knowledge of Learners

The teacher identifies and addresses the needs of learners by demonstrating respect for individual differences, cultures, backgrounds, and learning styles.

What Does the Research Say About Professional Knowledge of the Teacher?

Classroom teaching is a complex activity that demands that teachers possess substantial mental capacity and a solid knowledge base. Essential teacher knowledge ranges from content knowledge, to pedagogical knowledge, to curricular knowledge, to knowledge of learners, to knowledge of culture and educational purposes at large.

Content knowledge, the disciplinary understanding of the subject taught, exerts a significant influence on a teacher's classroom behavior. Various studies suggest that teachers with stronger content knowledge are more likely to use practices that can help students construct and internalize knowledge, such as:[2]

♦ Asking higher-level questions;

♦ Encouraging students to explore alternative explanations;

♦ Involving students in more inquiry learning;

♦ Allowing more student-directed activities;

♦ Better engaging students in the lessons.

Effective teaching resides not simply in the knowledge a teacher has accrued but in how this knowledge is translated into student learning in classrooms.[3] For instance, teachers highly proficient in mathematics or writing will help others learn mathematics or writing only if they are able to use their own knowledge to enact learning activities that are appropriate to students. Therefore, a teacher's subject-matter knowledge and pedagogical knowledge are complementary and interdependent. These two knowledge categories were synthesized by what Shulman called "pedagogical content knowledge," which he defined as "the blending of content and pedagogy into an understanding of how particular topics, problems, or issues are organized, represented, and adapted to the diverse interests and abilities of learners, and presented for instruction."[4]

Studies that examined the effects of a teacher's subject-matter knowledge and/or pedagogical knowledge on students' academic achievement often used simple survey questions and teachers' college course-taking and majors to measure teacher knowledge. Figure 2.3 (page 22) summarizes selected key studies that examined the association between teacher knowledge and student learning.

Figure 2.3. Key References for Effects of Teacher Subject-Matter Knowledge and Pedagogical Knowledge

Study	Knowledge Base Examined	Measured By	Grade Level	Subject(s)	Findings
Hill, Rowan, & Ball[5]	Content knowledge	Survey	Elementary	Mathematics	Teachers' mathematical knowledge significantly contributes to student mathematics learning, after controlling for other key student- and teacher-related characteristics.
Rowan, Chiang, & Miller[6]	Content knowledge	Survey and college major	High school	Mathematics	Students whose teachers answered the math quiz item correctly achieved more in mathematics than did those whose teachers answered the question wrong. Students whose teachers majored in mathematics at the undergraduate and/or graduate level achieved more than those whose teachers did not, although the effect was quite small (SD = 0.015).
Goldhaber & Brewer[7]	Content knowledge	College major	High school	Mathematics	Students learn more from teachers with majors in mathematics than students whose teachers had degrees in nonmathematics subjects.
Monk[8]	Content knowledge and pedagogical knowledge	College coursework	High school	Mathematics and science	The amount of college-level mathematics or science courses taken by teachers had a positive effect on student learning gains. The effects of pedagogical coursework are more stable over time than the effects of subject matter preparation.

A research synthesis by Rice concluded that coursework in both pedagogy and content area has a positive impact on student achievement in middle and high school education, primarily for mathematics.[9] Pedagogical coursework seems to contribute to teacher effectiveness at both elementary and secondary levels, but the importance of content coursework appears to be more salient at the secondary level. Although the impact of teacher content knowledge on student achievement has been indeterminate and inconsistent in nonmathematics subjects and at the elementary level, this does not necessarily mean there is no association between content knowledge and achievement. Consequently, more fine-tuned instruments need to be developed to measure teacher job-related knowledge and its effects on student achievement.[10]

Teaching knowledge of effective teachers reaches beyond the knowledge of subject matter (content knowledge) and teaching strategies (pedagogical knowledge); it also encompasses an understanding of students and environmental contexts.[11] Good teachers often use their knowledge of their students—for instance, knowledge of students' learning ability, prior achievement, cultural background, personal interests—to decide what to teach and how to teach. Based on this expansive knowledge, teachers can anticipate the conceptions, misconceptions, and possible difficulties their students are likely to encounter while learning particular content.

What Are Research-Based Quality Indicators for Professional Knowledge?

As indicated in Chapter 1, quality indicators are used to do just what the term implies—*indicate*, in observable behaviors, the types and quality of performance associated with a given performance standard, in this instance, with the *Professional Knowledge* performance standard. Quality indicators are tangible behaviors that can be observed or documented to determine the degree to which a teacher is fulfilling the *Professional Knowledge* performance standard.

Although the set of eight performance standards is provided as a comprehensive description of a teacher's key responsibilities, the quality indicators that rest underneath a given performance standard are merely examples. Figures 2.4 and 2.5, on page 24, are two sample lists of quality indicators for *professional knowledge*, but bear in mind that the quality indicators selected for the lists are only examples.

Figure 2.4. Sample 1: Quality Indicators for Professional Knowledge

The teacher

- effectively addresses appropriate curriculum standards.

- integrates key content elements and higher-level thinking skills in instruction.

- demonstrates ability to link present content with past and future learning experiences, other subject areas, and real-world experiences and applications.

- demonstrates accurate knowledge of the subject matter.

- demonstrates skills relevant to the subject area(s) taught.

- bases instruction on goals that reflect high expectations and understanding of the subject.

- understands intellectual, social, emotional, and physical development of the age group.

Figure 2.5. Sample 2: Quality Indicators for Professional Knowledge

The Curriculum

The teacher

- effectively addresses appropriate curriculum standards.

- integrates key content elements and higher-level thinking skills in instruction.

- links present content with past and upcoming learning experiences, other subject areas, and real-world experiences and applications.

Subject Content

The teacher

- demonstrates accurate knowledge of the subject matter.

- demonstrates skills relevant to the subject area(s) taught.

- bases instruction on goals that reflect high expectations and understanding of the subject.

Developmental Needs of Students

The teacher

- demonstrates an understanding of the intellectual, social, emotional, and physical developmental of the age group.

- uses appropriate school, family, and community resources to help meet all students' learning needs.

How Can Professional Knowledge Be Documented?

The *Professional Knowledge* performance standard and related quality indicators describe *what is expected* of a teacher for quality work. However, it isn't enough to know what is expected; we also must know *how to document* that the work is being done.

Historically, teacher work has been documented primarily, if not exclusively, through classroom observation. Observation does play an important role for documenting teachers' work for most performance standards, but is not the exclusive method. As Figure 2.6 indicates, both observation and portfolios/data logs are highlighted as valued information sources for accurately documenting the *Professional Knowledge* performance standard.[†]

Figure 2.6. Aligning Data Sources with the
Professional Knowledge Standard

Performance Standard	Observation	Portfolio/Data Log	Other Data Sources
Professional Knowledge	P	P	TBD

Note: P = primary data source; S = secondary data source; TBD = to be determined.

In the case of *professional knowledge,* both observations and portfolios/data logs can serve as primary data sources. Figure 2.7 is an abbreviated observation sample and Figure 2.8 (page 27) is a set of possible artifacts for inclusion in a portfolio/data log.

---

† Additional information sources (i.e., student surveys, measures of student progress) are detailed in other books recommended in the *Want to Know More* section in Part II.

Figure 2.7. Sample Classroom Observation Form for Professional Knowledge

Classroom Observation Form*

Teacher: _____ School:_____

Date:_____ Time:_____

Contract Status: ☐ Induction ☐ Continuing

Pre-Conference held ☐ No ☐ Yes, date _____

Type of Observation ☐ Formal ☐ Informal ☐ Walkthrough

Observer _____

This observation form focuses on established teacher performance. A copy of the completed observation form is to be given to the teacher.

Standard 1: *Professional Knowledge*	SPECIFIC EXAMPLES:
Quality Indicators ♦ Appropriate curriculum standards ♦ Key concepts are integrated ♦ Higher-order thinking skills ♦ Relationship to past/future ♦ Accurate knowledge ♦ High expectations ♦ Knowledge of development	

* This is an abbreviated version of a comprehensive classroom observation form provided in Part II of the book. For illustration purposes, the selected quality indicators may vary from those provided in the chapter.

Figure 2.8. Suggested Set of Artifacts to Include in a Portfolio/Data Log for Professional Knowledge

Professional Knowledge Artifacts

- Summary of a plan for integrating instruction

- Class profile

- Annotated list of instructional activities for a unit

- Annotated photographs of teacher-made displays used in instruction

- Annotated samples or photographs of instructional materials created by the teacher

- Lesson/intervention plan (including goals and objectives, activities, resources, and assessment measures)

- Summary of consultation with appropriate staff members regarding special needs of individual students

- Products of collaboration with colleagues or other professionals

- Journals that represent reflective thinking and professional growth

- Other artifacts as appropriate for the particular assignment or situation of the teacher

What Are Rating Scale Options for Professional Knowledge?

As noted in Chapter 1, rating scales are used to determine the effectiveness of performance (e.g., "meets standard," "does not meet standard"). However, rating scales, alone, are too prone to subjectivity. A solution to this limitation of rating scales is to design and consistently apply a performance appraisal rubric to the judgment of *how well* the performance standard has been fulfilled.

Figures 2.9, 2.10, and 2.11 (page 29) provide field-tested performance appraisal rubrics for the *Professional Knowledge* performance standard. The full sets of rubrics are provided in Part II.

Figure 2.9. Three-Point Performance Rubric for Professional Knowledge

Proficient*	Developing/Needs Improvement	Unsatisfactory
The teacher demonstrates an understanding of the curriculum, subject content, and the developmental needs of students.	The teacher inconsistently demonstrates understanding in the area(s) of curriculum, content, or student development; or inconsistently uses the knowledge for effective instruction.	The teacher bases instruction on information that is inaccurate or out-of-date and/or inadequately addresses the developmental needs of students.

* "Proficient" is the baseline of acceptable performance for teachers and is the actual performance standard.

Figure 2.10. Four-Point Performance Rubric for Professional Knowledge

Exemplary *In addition to meeting the standard…*	Proficient*	Developing/ Needs Improvement	Unsatisfactory
The teacher consistently demonstrates extensive knowledge of the subject matter and continually enriches the curriculum.	The teacher demonstrates an understanding of the curriculum, subject content, and the developmental needs of students by providing relevant learning experiences.	The teacher inconsistently demonstrates understanding of curriculum, content, and student development or lacks fluidity of using the knowledge in practice.	The teacher bases instruction on material that is inaccurate or out-of-date and/or inadequately addresses the developmental needs of students.

* "Proficient" is the baseline of acceptable performance for teachers and is the actual performance standard.

Figure 2.11. Five-Point Performance Rubric for Professional Knowledge

Exemplary _The professional's work is exceptional. In addition to meeting the standard..._	Superior _In addition to meeting the standard..._	Proficient _The description is the actual performance standard._	Developing/Needs Improvement	Unsatisfactory
The teacher consistently plays a leadership role by integrating knowledge of learners to address the needs of the target learning community.	The teacher often meets the individual and diverse needs of learners in a highly effective manner.	The teacher identifies and addresses the needs of learners by demonstrating respect for individual differences, cultures, backgrounds, and learning styles.	The teacher attempts, but is often ineffective in demonstrating knowledge and understanding of the needs of the target learning community.	The teacher consistently demonstrates a lack of awareness of the needs of the target learning community or does not consistently make appropriate accommodations to meet those needs.

Notes

1 Harris, D. N., & Sass, T. R. (2007); Hill, H. C., Rowan, B., & Ball, D. L. (2005); Rowan, B., Chiang, F. S., & Miller, R. J. (1997).

2 Weiss, I. R., & Miller, B. (2006, October); Wenglisky, H. (2000).

3 Hill, H. C., Rowan, B., & Ball, D. L. (2005).

4 Shulman, L. S. (1987). p. 8.

5 Hill, H. C., Rowan, B., & Ball, D. L. (2005).

6 Rowan, B., Chiang, F. S., & Miller, R. J. (1997).

7 Goldhaber, D. D., & Brewer, D. J. (1997); Goldhaber, D. D., & Brewer, D. J. (2000).

8 Monk, D. H. (1994).

9 Rice, J. K. (2003).

10 Rowan, B., Schilling, S. G., Ball, D. L., & Miller, R. (2001, October).

11 Cochran, K., DeRuiter, L., & King, R. (1993).

3

Data-Driven Planning

A teacher's teaching begins before the teacher steps into the classroom and starts talking. Prior to each lesson, unit, semester, or school year, while teachers are planning the content of instruction, selecting teaching materials, designing the learning activities and grouping methods, and deciding on the pacing and allocation of instructional time, they are actually determining what learning opportunities their students are going to have. Teachers could use state or district curriculum standards, school district curriculum goals and objectives, and learning outcomes developed by professional organizations to plot the scope and sequence of subject topics. Teachers also could apply their knowledge of research-based practices to plan what strategies and techniques will be adopted to deliver instruction. Nevertheless, the most informative source for any instructional planning resides in the teachers' classrooms—the students. This chapter explores the teacher performance standard of data-driven planning. The questions addressed in this chapter include:

- What does *data-driven planning* mean?
- What does the research say about *data-driven planning*?
- What are research-based quality indicators for *data-driven planning*?
- How can *data-driven planning* be documented?
- What are rating scale options for *data-driven planning*?

What Does *Data-Driven Planning* Mean?

In general terms, planning means the "act or process of making or carrying out plans."[1] The real question for our purposes, however, is addressing the "data-driven" aspects of planning and then applying the generic process of planning more specifically to teachers' work.

Data-Driven Aspects of Planning

In terms of using data in planning, a central concern to consider is the proper use of proper data. It appears that we have become so enamored in recent years with the idea of data that wild, unsubstantiated, and largely useless claims of "data-driven decision making" loosely circulate in educational circles. The sentiment for using data wisely is nicely described in a thoughtful *Educational Leadership* article:

A decade or so ago, it was disconcertingly easy to find education leaders who dismissed student achievement data and systematic research as having only limited utility when it came to improving schools or school systems. Today, we have come full circle: It is hard to attend an education conference or read an education journal without encountering broad claims for data-based decision making and research-based practice....Yet these phrases can too readily morph into convenient buzzwords that obscure rather than clarify. Indeed, I fear that both "data-based decision making" and "research-based practice" can stand in for careful thought, serve as dressed-up rationales for the same old fads, or be used to justify incoherent proposals.[2]

Simply claiming "data-based" doesn't improve practice. Rather, we must:

♦ Gather pertinent data (i.e., quantitative and qualitative information);

♦ Distill the real meaning of these data (i.e., What does the information tell us about teaching and learning?);

♦ Aptly apply the information to improve and sustain good practice, and then;

♦ Improve results.

"Data-Driven decision making does not simply require good data; it also requires good decisions."[3]

Applying Planning Processes to Teaching

Planning is preparation for action. Without prior thought and planning, ongoing review and adjustment as the plan unfolds in practice, and, finally, reflection on what worked, what didn't, and how to improve, we seldom improve practice. Indeed, planning is an essential tool for effective teaching. In applying planning concepts and processes to teaching, various research studies have found that effective teachers are more likely to have the planning behaviors summarized in Figure 3.1 while deciding on subject content.

Figure 3.1. Key Aspects of Data-Driven Planning for Effective Teachers

♦ Construct a blueprint of how to address the curriculum during the instructional time.[4]

♦ Facilitate planning units in advance to make intra- and interdisciplinary connections.[5]

♦ Collaborate with one or more teachers while planning, rather than plan lessons alone.[6]

♦ Use student assessment data to plan what goals and objectives to address.[7]

♦ Plan for the context of the lesson to help students relate, organize, and make knowledge become a part of students' long-term memory.[8]

- Sequence material to promote student's cognitive and developmental growth.[9]
- Use knowledge of available resources to determine what resources they need to acquire or develop.[10]
- Plan instruction in a multisourced manner.[11]

Definitions of Data-Driven Planning

Figure 3.2 provides two sample definitions for *data-driven planning*. These definitions can be used to help operationalize the teacher performance standard, *Data-Driven Planning*.

Figure 3.2. Sample Definitions for the *Data-Driven Planning* Performance Standard

Sample 1. Data-Driven Planning

The teacher plans for the use of appropriate curricula, instructional strategies, and resources to address the needs of all students by applying pertinent evidence of student learning.

Sample 2: Instructional Planning

The teacher uses appropriate curricula, instructional strategies, and resources during the planning process to address the diverse needs of students.

What Does the Research Say About Data-Driven Planning?

The Process of Planning

Instructional planning is a deliberate process that teachers deploy. Figure 3.3 lists key questions to consider in the process of planning.

Figure 3.3 Key Questions to Consider in Instructional Planning

- What should be taught?
- How should it be taught?
- How should instruction and student learning be assessed?

What Should Be Taught?

Effective student learning requires a progressive and coherent set of learning objectives. State/provincial/national standards and school district curriculum can point out the generic domains of subject content to be covered. However, it is the teacher's responsibility in virtually every classroom to delineate the intended outcomes of each lesson and describe the behaviors or actions that students should be able to perform after participating in the learning activities.

In deciding what should be taught, expert teachers often do dip into prescribed textbooks, but they hardly ever follow traditional plans. In fact, they frequently have a blueprint in their minds that has been formed and reformed over time. Perhaps because of their expertise gained over time through a constant process of planning–reflection–refining, these expert teachers are more prone to rely far less on written, formalized lessons than on their well-formed and fluid mental planning model.[12]

Additionally, as effective teachers consider what to teach, they typically reach beyond prepared materials. For instance, while planning for a lesson in social science, effective teachers usually use historical fiction, biography, information on the Internet and in magazines, and other nontraditional content sources. Leinhardt found that expert teachers and novice teachers have different "agenda" for their daily instruction.[13] Agenda is defined as an operational plan that is concise, focused, and descriptive of the intended goals and actions in which the teacher seeks to engage the students during the instructional time. Particularly, Leinhardt noticed that expert teachers conceive a lesson along two dimensions simultaneously:

1. Teacher's own actions, thoughts, and habits; and

2. Students' thinking and understanding of the content.

Thus, effective teachers not only plan what to teach, but more importantly, they plan who they are going to teach. They exert efforts to reach beyond their comfort zone of disciplinary thinking and actions to incorporate their students' learning preferences.

How Should It Be Taught?

Once the learning objectives are developed, evidence suggests that expert teachers are more competent in translating their instructional plans into actions than nonexpert teachers.[14] Additionally, effective teachers follow the predefined plan while remaining open to changes and continuously adjusting their instruction based on student needs. Furthermore, expert teachers anticipate the difficulties students might encounter while learning the content of the lesson, and consider students' thinking in order to assess the success of the lesson plan and then modify their instruction promptly.[15]

Having a lesson plan cannot ensure that the actual lesson will be implemented as what's prescribed. Human behavior, either of the teachers or of the students in the classroom, cannot be predicted accurately as a phenomenon in the hard sciences. As any good teacher or administrator knows, the classroom is full of ebbs and flows. Consequently, teachers need to tap into their pedagogical and content resources in a fluid and flexible manner in order to proceed smoothly—and successfully.

How Should Instruction and Student Learning Be Assessed?

When the learning objectives are set up, in addition to aligning activities to them, teachers also need to link the assessment plan to the learning objective. Alignment of curriculum, learning activities, and assessment is integral to any instructional design. (This type of alignment is referred to as "opportunity to learn.") Before the actual instruction starts, teachers need to decide upon valid and reliable assessment techniques that are available to solicit student learning data and judge the success of the instructional plan. Additionally, teachers should communicate to their students about what they are expected to achieve and inform them about how they will be assessed after participating in the learning activities.

Pacing Guides as a Planning Tool*

Teachers must consider a variety of factors when planning instruction, including how to pace the actual delivery in the classroom. The feasibility of a particular lesson largely depends on student ability and variation, content goals and mandated objectives, time and material resources, and so forth. Many of these factors present teachers with constraints that are beyond their immediate control. For example, there is a prescribed, fixed amount of time each day in which formal instruction may occur. Typically, hours of the day are chunked into units that are dedicated to the study of a certain subject or discipline as determined by a legislative body, school board, or even a school administrator. Within those chunks of time, however, teachers have traditionally enjoyed a great deal of flexibility and autonomy. That is, what they did with class time was largely up to them. Over the past decade that flexibility has begun to wane—a by-product of high-stakes testing. Teachers report a narrowing of the curriculum that focuses on tested items and breadth of content while sacrificing depth.[16]

Many school districts require teachers to follow strict pacing guides that prescribe how much time to spend on certain lessons or concepts. Pacing guides are intended to be instruments that teachers use to measure the amount of instructional time devoted to certain topics in light of the total content that must be taught. Properly used, pacing guides are tools to steer daily instructional decisions within the context of the entire curriculum. Used improperly, however, pacing guides unduly restrict the proper ebb and flow of the classroom and restrict the instructional pace regardless of student ability. On this topic, one writer stated:[17]

> Pacing guides are not an inherently bad idea. Their effects depend on their design and how district and school leaders use them. The best pacing guides emphasize curriculum guidance instead of prescriptive pacing; these guides focus on central ideas and provide links to exemplary curriculum material, lessons, and instructional strategies.

Thus, pacing, if used wisely, can be an important component of instructional planning. It allows teachers to see the curriculum in its entirety and avoid the trap of overempha-

---

* This section is adapted from Robert Williams' unpublished paper. Mr. Williams is a doctoral student in Educational Policy, Planning, and Leadership, the College of William and Mary.

sizing one area of content at the expense of others. And, because instructional time with students is fixed, teachers must value class time; pacing can help with this important planning consideration.

What Are Research-Based Quality Indicators for Data-Driven Planning?

As indicated in Chapter 1, quality indicators are used to do just what the term implies—*indicate,* in observable behaviors, the types and quality of performance associated with a given performance standard, in this instance, with the *Data-Driven Planning* performance standard. Quality indicators are tangible behaviors that can be observed or documented to determine the degree to which a teacher is fulfilling the *Data-Driven Planning* performance standard.

Although the set of eight performance standards highlighted in the book is provided as a comprehensive description of a teacher's key responsibilities, the quality indicators that rest underneath a given performance standard are merely *examples*. Figures 3.4 and 3.5 are two sample lists of quality indicators for *data-driven planning*, but bear in mind that the quality indicators selected for the lists are only examples.

Figure 3.4. Sample 1 of Quality Indicators for Data-Driven Planning

The teacher

♦ develops plans that are clear, logical, sequential, and integrated across the curriculum (e.g., long-term goals, lesson plans, and syllabi).

♦ matches content/skills taught to overall curriculum scope and sequence.

♦ evaluates curricular materials for accuracy, currency, and student interest.

♦ designs coherent instruction based upon knowledge of subject matter, students, the community, and curriculum standards and goals.

♦ demonstrates the ability to evaluate and refine existing materials and to create new materials when necessary.

♦ identifies and plans for the instructional and developmental needs of all students, including remedial, high achievers, and identified gifted students.

Figure 3.5. Sample 2 of Quality Indicators for Data-Driven Planning

The teacher

♦ identifies and plans differentiated instruction to meet the needs of *all* students (e.g., students with disabilities, high-achieving and identified gifted students, English language learners).

♦ develops plans that are clear, logical, sequential, and integrated across the curriculum—long-term goals, lesson plans and syllabi (pacing guide).

♦ matches content/skills taught to overall curriculum scope and sequence.

- ♦ evaluates and modifies *curricular* materials for accuracy, timeliness, and student interest.

- ♦ evaluates and modifies *instructional* materials for accuracy, timeliness, and student interest.

- ♦ designs coherent instruction based upon appropriate knowledge of subject matter, students, the community, and curriculum standards and goals.

- ♦ ensures substitute lesson plans are timely, appropriate, clear, and accompanied by needed resources.

How Can Data-Driven Planning Be Documented?

The *Data-Driven Planning* performance standard and related quality indicators describe *what is expected* of a teacher for quality work. However, it isn't enough to know what is expected; we also must know *how to document* that the work is being done.

Historically, teacher work has been documented primarily, if not exclusively, through classroom observation. Observation does play an important role for documenting teachers' work for most performance standards, but is not the exclusive method. As Figure 3.6 indciates, both observation and portfolios/data logs are valued information sources for accurately documenting the *Data-Driven Planning* performance standard.[†]

Figure 3.6. Aligning Data Sources with the Data-Driven Planning Standard

Performance Standard	Observation	Portfolio/Data Log	Other Data Sources
Data-Driven Planning	S	P	TBD

Note: P = primary data source; S = secondary data source; TBD = to be determined.

In the case of *Data-Driven Planning*, portfolios/data logs often serve as a primary data source while observation serves more as a secondary source. Figure 3.7 is an abbreviated observation sample and Figure 3.8 is a set of possible artifacts for inclusion in a portfolio/data log.

---

† Additional information sources (i.e., student surveys, measures of student progress) are detailed in other books recommended in the "Want to Know More" section in Part II of the book.

Figure 3.7. Abbreviated Classroom Form for Data-Driven Planning

Classroom Observation Form*

Teacher: _____   School:_____

Date:_____   Time:_____

Contract Status: ☐ Induction ☐ Continuing

Pre-Conference held ☐ No   ☐ Yes, date _____

Type of Observation ☐ Formal   ☐ Informal   ☐ Walkthrough

Observer _____

This observation form focuses on established teacher performance. A copy of the completed observation form is to be given to the teacher.

Standard 1: *Data-Driven Planning*	SPECIFIC EXAMPLES:
Quality Indicators ♦ Clear, logical plans integrated with state and local curriculum guides ♦ Selection of differentiated strategies ♦ Guiding questions identified ♦ Coherent instructional plans ♦ Curriculum materials ♦ Learning needs are accommodated ♦ Student performance expectations identified ♦ Plans address short- and long-range goals	

* This is an abbreviated version of a comprehensive classroom observation form provided in Part II of the book. For illustration purposes, the selected quality indicators may vary from those provided in the chapter.

**Figure 3.8. Suggested Set of Artifacts to Include in a
Portfolio/Data Log for Data-Driven Planning**

Data-Driven Planning Artifacts

- Sample lesson or unit plan related to the pre- and postassessment
- Summary of a plan for integrating instruction
- Course syllabus
- Intervention plan
- Substitute lesson plan
- Annotated list of learning objectives for a unit/semester
- Annotated list of learning activities
- Annotated samples of learning materials
- Products of collaborative planning with colleagues

What Are Rating Scale Options for Data-Driven Planning?

As noted in Chapter 1, rating scales are used to determine the effectiveness of performance (i.e., "meets standard," "does not meet standard"). However, rating scales, alone, are too prone to subjectivity. A solution to this limitation of rating scales is to design and consistently apply a performance appraisal rubric to the judgment of *how well* the performance standard has been fulfilled.

Figures 3.9, 3.10 (page 40), and 3.11 (page 40) provide field-tested performance appraisal rubrics for the *Data-Driven Planning* performance standard. Full sets of rubrics are provided in Part II of the book.

Figure 3.9. Three-Point Performance Rubric for Data-Driven Planning

Proficient*	Needs Improvement	Unsatisfactory
The teacher plans for the use of appropriate curricula, instructional strategies and resources to address the needs of *all* students.	The teacher inconsistently uses appropriate curricula, instructional strategies, and resources during the planning process to address the needs of all students.	The teacher rarely uses appropriate curricula, instructional strategies, and resources during the planning process to address the needs of students.

* "Proficient" is the baseline of acceptable performance for teachers and is the actual performance standard.

Figure 3.10. Four-Point Performance Rubric for Data-Driven Planning

Exemplary In addition to meeting the standard…	Proficient*	Needs Improvement	Unsatisfactory
The teacher's planning process consistently anticipates student misconceptions and/or prior knowledge by employing a variety of instructional strategies and resources.	The teacher's planning uses appropriate curricula, instructional strategies, and resources to address the needs of all students.	The teacher's planning displays inconsistent use of curricula, strategies, and/or resources to meet students' needs.	The teacher's planning inadequately meets the needs of the learners and/or follows the adopted curriculum.

* "Proficient" is the baseline of acceptable performance for teachers and is the actual performance standard.

Figure 3.11. Five-Point Performance Rubric for Data-Driven Planning

Exemplary The professional's work is exceptional. In addition to meeting the standard…	Superior In addition to meeting the standard…	Proficient The description is the actual performance standard.	Developing/Needs Improvement	Unsatisfactory
The teacher consistently creates standards-based curricula and evaluates appropriate curricula, instructional strategies, and resources to plan and modify instruction in order to address the diverse needs of students.	The teacher often uses appropriate curricula, instructional strategies, and resources to plan, modify, and adjust instruction in order to meet the diverse needs of students.	The teacher uses appropriate curricula, instructional strategies, and resources during the planning process, including state reading requirements, to address the diverse needs of students.	The teacher attempts to use appropriate curricula, instructional strategies, and/or resources during the planning process, but is often ineffective in meeting the diverse needs of all learners.	The teacher consistently demonstrates a lack of planning or does not properly address the curriculum in meeting the diverse needs of all learners.

Notes

1   Merriam-Webster, Inc. (2006). p. 1387.

2   Hess, F. M. (2008, December/ 2009, January). p. 12.

3   Hess, F. M. (2008, December/ 2009, January), p. 17.

4   McEwan, E. K. (2002).

5   McEwan, E. K. (2002).

6   Haynie, G. (2006, April).

7   Haynie, G. (2006, April).

8   Marzano, R. J., Pickering, D. & McTighe, J. (1993).

9   Panasuk, R., Stone, W., & Todd, J. (2002).

10   Buttram, J. L., & Waters, J. T. (1997).

11   Allington, R. L., & Johnston, P. H. (2000).

12   See for example, Stronge, J. H., Little, C., & Grant, L. W. (2008, July16).

13   Leinhardt, G. (1993).

14   Borko, H., & Livingston, C. (1989).

15   Leinhardt, G. (1993).

16   Au, W. (2007).

17   David, J. L. (2008). p. 88.

4

Instructional Delivery

The primary difference between effective and ineffective teachers does not lie in the amount of knowledge they have about disciplinary content,[1] the type of certificate they hold,[2] the highest degree they earned,[3] or the years they have been in the teaching profession;[4] rather, the difference lies more fundamentally in the manner in which they deliver their knowledge and skills while interacting with the students in their classroom.[5] Numerous studies reveal that schools and teachers with the same resources yield different results in terms of student learning. Thus, it seems clear that these differences depend on how the resources are used by those who work in instruction.[6] This chapter addresses the following five questions related to the teacher's important work in instructional delivery:

- ◆ What does *instructional delivery* mean?
- ◆ What does the research say about *instructional delivery*?
- ◆ What are research-based quality indicators for *instructional delivery*?
- ◆ How can *instructional delivery* be documented?
- ◆ What are rating scale options for *instructional delivery*?

What Does *Instructional Delivery* Mean?

Instructional delivery is a process in which teachers apply a repertoire of instructional strategies, to communicate and interact with students around academic content, and to support student engagement. An array of studies reveal that teachers who have similar background in the highest degree obtained or teaching experience instruct differently in their classroom and vary significantly in their ability to help students grow academically.[7] Instructional delivery, among various teacher characteristics, undoubtedly is among the most crucial factor that matters for student learning. Teachers' instruction has the most proximal relation with student learning, while teacher background qualifications and other educational inputs can, at most, influence learning indirectly through their association with teacher instructional performance.[8] To elaborate, Figure 4.1 highlights some key areas of instructional delivery.

Figure 4.1. Key Areas of Instructional Delivery for Effective Teachers

Area	Focus
Differentiation	The teacher uses multiple instructional materials, activities, strategies, and assessment techniques to meet students' needs and maximize the learning of all students.[9]
Cognitive challenge	The teacher provides in-depth explanations of academic content and covers higher-order concepts and skills thoroughly.[10]
Student engagement	The teacher is supportive and persistent in keeping students on task and encouraging them to actively integrate new information with prior learning.[11]
Questioning	The teacher uses multiples levels (particularly higher cognitive levels) of questioning to stimulate student thinking and monitor student learning.[12]
Relevance	The learning process and the outcomes of learning have authentic "bearing" on students' life.[13]

Figure 4.2 provides two sample definitions for *instructional delivery*. These definitions can be used to help operationalize the teacher performance standard, *Instructional Delivery*.

Figure 4.2. Sample Definitions for the Instructional Delivery Performance Standard

Sample 1. Instructional Delivery

The teacher promotes student learning by addressing individual learning differences and by using effective instructional strategies.

Sample 2. Instructional Delivery and Engagement

The teacher promotes learning by demonstrating accurate content knowledge and by addressing academic needs through a variety of appropriate instructional strategies and technologies that engage learners.

What Does the Research Say About Instructional Delivery?

Students arrive at school with a variety of backgrounds, interests, and abilities. This means that a one-size-fits-all approach to instruction is ineffective, probably counterproductive, and perhaps even unethical. If the goal of instruction is to provide an opportunity for all students to learn, then the instructional practices that teachers choose to employ in the classroom matter—and matter greatly.[14] In an analysis of educational productivity in the United States and other countries, teacher classroom instruction was identified as one of the most significant variables that has great effect on student affective, behavioral, and cognitive outcomes.[15] Good quality instruction positively and directly affects student achievement. For instance, the instructional practice of reinforcement has a magnitude of 1.17 standard deviations on educational outcomes. And the effect of cues, engagement, and corrective feedback, each, is approximately one standard deviation. Personalized and adaptive instruction, tutoring, and diagnostic-prescriptive methods also have strong effects on student learning, with effect sizes of 0.57, 0.45, 0.40, and 0.33, respectively.[16]

Instead of using uniform strategies for all students, effective teachers design instruction that motivates each student and they communicate content in such a way that students are able to comprehend based on their individual prior learning and ability. Because students learn in a variety of ways and at a variety of rates, teachers should deliver their lessons with appropriate variety. A meta-analysis of the extant research suggests that instruction based on learning styles is positively related to student attitudes and achievement.[17] Dunn et al. extended this finding to at-risk students, reporting that mean achievement increased nearly one standard deviation (i.e., approximately 84th percentile vs. 50th percentile) when teachers accommodated for learning styles.[18] Implementing a variety of classroom techniques and strategies also enhances student motivation and decreases discipline problems.[19] Furthermore, differentiated instruction enables teachers to adjust their curriculum, materials, learning activities, and assessment techniques to ensure that all students in a mixed-ability classroom can have different avenues to process new knowledge and develop skills, while having equal access to high-quality learning.[20]

Making instruction relevant to real-world problems is among the most powerful instructional practices a teacher can use to increase student learning.[21] This kind of instruction allows students to explore, inquire, and meaningfully construct knowledge of real problems that are relevant to their life. Moreover, students are motivated and engaged when their learning is authentic, especially when the real-world tasks performed have personalized results.

Questioning can be another highly effective instructional tool when used properly. In particular, the types of questions asked, wait time, and types of responses play a role in the propitious use of questioning. Unfortunately, there are substantial differences in the adept use of questioning between effective teachers and ineffective teachers. On the negative side, in a study of mathematics classrooms Craig and Cairo found that teachers ask more than 99 percent of the questions.[22] They also found that teachers tended to provide little wait time, asked recall and use questions, and designated a particular student to answer a question. On the positive side, in one case study the researchers found that teachers deemed effective asked approximately seven times more higher cognitive-level questions than those considered ineffective.[23] Figure 4.3 identifies selected instructional practices exhibited by effective teachers.

**Figure 4.3. Selected Instructional Practices
Employed by Effective Teachers**

The effective teacher

♦ stays involved with the lesson at all stages so that adjustments can be made based on feedback from the students.[24]

♦ uses a variety of instructional strategies, as no one strategy is universally superior with all students.[25]

♦ uses research-based strategies to enhance the time students spend with teachers by making instruction student centered.[26]

♦ involves students in cooperative learning to enhance higher-order thinking skills.[27]

♦ knows that instructional strategies that use students' prior knowledge in an inquiry-based, hands-on format facilitates student learning.[28]

♦ uses remediation, skills-based instruction, and individualized instruction to differentiate for individual student's needs.[29]

♦ uses multiple levels of questioning aligned with students' cognitive abilities with appropriate techniques.[30]

There is no single classroom practice that is necessarily effective with all subject matter and all grade levels.[31] Effective instruction involves a dynamic interplay among content to be learned, pedagogical method applied, characteristics of individual learners, and the context in which the learning is to occur.[32] Ultimately, subject matter knowledge, pedagogical skills, and an inspiration for instructional innovation and development can liberate individual teachers to explore the diversification and richness of daily practice.

What Are Research-Based Quality Indicators for Instructional Delivery?

As indicated in Chapter 1, quality indicators are used to do just what the term implies— *indicate*, in observable behaviors, the types and quality of performance associated with a given performance standard, in this instance, the *Instructional Delivery* performance standard. Quality indicators are tangible behaviors that can be observed or documented to determine the degree to which a teacher is fulfilling the *Instructional Delivery* performance standard.

Although the set of eight performance standards in the book is provided as a comprehensive description of a teacher's key responsibilities, the quality indicators that rest underneath a given performance standard are merely *examples*. Figures 4.4 and 4.5 are two sample lists of quality indicators for *Instructional Delivery*, but bear in mind that the quality indicators selected for the lists are only examples.

Figure 4.4. Sample 1 of Quality Indicators for Instructional Delivery

The teacher

◆ modifies instruction to make topics relevant to students' lives and experiences.

◆ engages students in individual work, cooperative learning, and whole-group activities.

◆ uses materials, technology, and resources to provide learning experiences that challenge, motivate, and actively involve the learner.

◆ uses a variety of appropriate teaching strategies, which may include grouping, cooperative, peer and project-based learning, audiovisual presentations, lecture, discussions and inquiry, practice and application, and questioning, and the like.

◆ paces instruction appropriately with adequate preview and review of instructional components.

◆ solicits comments, questions, examples, and other contributions from students throughout lessons.

◆ integrates available technology in the classroom.

◆ demonstrates ability to engage and maintain students' attention and to recapture or refocus it as necessary.

Figure 4.5. Sample 2 of Quality Indicators for Instructional Delivery

The teacher

◆ incorporates a variety of research-based teaching methods and instructional strategies in lessons.

◆ uses appropriate materials, technology, and resources.

◆ provides learning experiences that engage, challenge, motivate, and actively involve the learner.

◆ teaches essential knowledge and develops students' critical thinking and problem-solving skills.

◆ makes learning relevant by connecting students' prior knowledge and experiences to the learning process.

◆ delivers instruction in a culturally, linguistically, and gender-sensitive manner.

◆ differentiates instruction based on individual needs of *all* students (e.g., students with disabilities, high-achieving and identified gifted students, special education, English language learners).

How Can Instructional Delivery Be Documented?

The *Instructional Delivery* performance standard and related quality indicators describe *what is expected* of a teacher for quality work. However, it isn't enough to know what is expected; we also must know *how to document* that the work is being done.

Historically, teacher work has been documented primarily, if not exclusively, through classroom observation. Observation does play an important role for documenting teachers' work for most performance standards, but is not the exclusive method. As Figure 4.6 indicates, both observation and portfolios/data logs are highlighted as valued information sources for accurately documenting the *Instructional Delivery* performance standard.*

Figure 4.6. Aligning Data Sources with the Instructional Delivery Standard

Performance Standard	Observation	Portfolio/Data Log	Other Data Sources
Instructional Delivery	P	S	TBD

Note: P = primary data source; S = secondary data source; TBD = to be determined.

In the case of instructional delivery, observations tend to serve as a primary data source and portfolios/data logs as a supplemental, or secondary, data source. An abbreviated observation sample (Figure 4.7) and a set of possible artifacts for inclusion in a portfolio/data log (Figure 4.8) are provided here.

Figure 4.7. Aligning Data Sources with the Instructional Delivery Standard

Classroom Observation Form*

Teacher: _____   School:_____

Date:_____ Time:_____

Contract Status: ☐ Induction ☐ Continuing

Pre-Conference held ☐ No ☐ Yes, date _____

Type of Observation ☐ Formal   ☐ Informal   ☐ Walkthrough

Observer _____

---

* Additional information sources (i.e., student surveys, measures of student progress) are detailed in other books recommended in the "Want to Know More" section in Part II of the book.

This observation form focuses on established teacher performance. A copy of the completed observation form is to be given to the teacher.

Standard 3: *Instructional Delivery*	SPECIFIC EXAMPLES:
Quality Indicators ♦ Variety of teaching methods, strategies, resources ♦ Effective pacing ♦ Student involvement ♦ Differentiation ♦ Relevance of instruction ♦ Technology use ♦ Essential knowledge, critical thinking, and problem solving	

* This is an abbreviated version of a comprehensive classroom observation form provided in Part II of the book. For illustration purposes, the selected quality indicators may vary from those provided in the chapter.

Figure 4.8. Suggested Set of Artifacts to Include in a Portfolio/Data Log for Instructional Delivery

Instructional Delivery Artifacts

♦ Summary of a plan for integrating instruction

♦ Annotated photographs of class activities

♦ Handouts/overhead samples

♦ Video/audio samples of instructional units

♦ Technology samples on disk

♦ Log of instructional time uses in classroom

♦ Annotated samples of instructional resources used in classroom

♦ Annotated sample of instructional strategies implemented in classroom

♦ Annotated sample of student learning products

♦ Student profiles used to make instructional decisions

♦ List of questions asked during instruction

♦ Reflective journal on current instructional performance and areas of improvement

What Are Rating Scale Options
for Instructional Delivery?

As noted in Chapter 1, rating scales are used to determine the effectiveness of performance (i.e., "meets standard," "does not meet standard"). However, rating scales, alone, are too prone to subjectivity. A solution to this limitation of rating scales is to design and consistently apply a performance appraisal rubric to the judgment of *how well* the performance standard has been fulfilled.

Figures 4.9, 4.10, and 4.11 provide field-tested performance appraisal rubrics for the *Instructional Delivery* performance standard. The full sets of rubrics are provided in Part II of the book.

Figure 4.9. Three-Point Performance Rubric for Instructional Delivery

Proficient*	Needs Improvement	Unsatisfactory
The teacher promotes student learning by addressing individual learning differences and by using effective instructional strategies.	The teacher inconsistently addresses individual learning differences and/or uses effective instructional strategies.	The teacher rarely delivers effective instruction.

* "Proficient" is the baseline of acceptable performance for teachers and is the actual performance standard.

Figure 4.10. Four-Point Performance Rubric for Instructional Delivery

Exemplary *In addition to meeting the standard…*	Proficient*	Needs Improvement	Unsatisfactory
The teacher's instructional delivery optimizes students' opportunity to learn by engaging students in higher-order thinking skills and processes to address divergent learning needs.	The teacher promotes student learning by addressing individual learning differences and by using effective instructional strategies.	The teacher inconsistently differentiates instruction and/or uses limited instructional strategies.	The teacher offers instruction that inadequately addresses differences in students' learning needs.

* "Proficient" is the baseline of acceptable performance for teachers and is the actual performance standard.

Figure 4.11. Five-Point Performance Rubric for Instructional Delivery

Exemplary *The professional's work is exceptional. In addition to meeting the standard…*	Superior *In addition to meeting the standard…*	Proficient *The description is the actual performance standard.*	Developing/Needs Improvement	Unsatisfactory
The teacher consistently optimizes learning by engaging all groups of students in higher-order thinking and by effectively implementing a variety of appropriate instructional strategies and technologies.	The teacher often promotes learning by addressing the academic needs of all groups of students at a high level, and by using a variety of appropriate instructional strategies and technologies.	The teacher promotes learning by demonstrating accurate content knowledge and by addressing academic needs through a variety of appropriate instructional strategies and technologies that engage learners.	The teacher attempts to use instructional strategies or technology to engage students, but is often ineffective or needs additional content knowledge.	The teacher lacks content knowledge or does not consistently implement instructional strategies to academically engage learners.

Notes

1 Harris, D. N., & Sass, T. R. (2007).

2 Rowan, B., Correnti, R., & Miller, R. J. (2002); Palardy, G. J., & Rumberger, R. W. (2008).

3 Hanushek, E. A., Kain, J. F., & Rivkin, S. G. (1998, August); Rivkin, S. G., Hanushek, E. A., & Kain, J. F. (2005).

4 Munoz, M. A., & Chang, F. C. (2007); Rockoff, J. E. (2004).

5 Bembry, K. L., Jordan, H. R., Gomez, E., Anderson, M. C., & Mendro, R. L. (1998, April); Hattie, J. (2003); Stronge, J. H., Ward, T. J., Tucker, P. D., & Hindman, J. L. (2008).

6 Cohen, D. K., Raudenbush, S. W., & Ball, D. L. (2003).

7 Rivkin, S. G., Hanushek, E. A., & Kain, J. F. (2005); Rowan, B., Correnti, R., & Miller, R. J. (2002); Stronge, J. H., Ward, T. J., Tucker, P. D., & Hindman, J. L. (2008).

8 Cohen, D. K., Raudenbush, S. W., & Ball, D. L. (2003); Palardy, G. J., & Rumberger, R. W. (2008).

9 Tomlinson, C. A. (1999).

10 Wenglinsky, H. (2002).

11 Cotton, K. (2000).

12 Cawelti, G. (2004); Walsh, J. A., & Sattes, B. D. (2005).

13 Schroeder, C. M., Scott, T. P., Tolson, H., Huang, T., & Lee, Y. (2007); Wenglinsky, H. (2004).

14 Carlson, E., Lee, H, & Schroll, K. (2004).

15 Walberg, H. J. (1984).

16 Walberg, H. J. (1984).

17 Lovelace, M. K. (2005).

18 Dunn, R., Honigsfeld, A., Shea Doolan, L., Bostrom, L., Russo, K., Schiering, M.S., et al. (2009).

19 Dolezal, S. E., Welsh, L. M., Pressley, M., & Vincent, M. M. (2003).

20 Tomlinson, C. A. (2001).

21 Schroeder, C. M., Scott, T. P., Tolson, H., Huang, T., & Lee, Y. (2007); Wenglinsky, H. J. (2004).

22 Craig, J., & Cairo, L. (2005, December).

23 Stronge, J. H., Ward, T. J., Tucker, P. D., & Hindman, J. L. (2008).

24 Education USA Special Report. (n. d.).

25 Darling-Hammond, L. (2001); Educational Review Office. (1998).

26 Johnson, B. L. (1997).

27 Shellard, E. & Protheroe, N. (2000).

28 Covino, E. A., & Iwanicki, E. (1996).

29 Shellard, E., & Protheroe, N. (2000).

30 Cawelti, G. (1999); Cotton, K. (2000); Covino E. A., & Iwanicki, E. (1996); Good, T. L., & Brophy, J. E. (1997); Tobin, K. (1980); Wang, M., Haertel, G. D., & Walberg, H. (1994).

31 McDonald, F. J., & Elias, P. (1976).

32 Schalock, H. D., Schalock, M. D., Cowart, B., & Myton, D. (1993).

5

Assessment for Learning

When we think about a teacher's performance in assessment of student learning, it must be more than merely testing students, as well as more than measuring achievement. In fact, teacher skill in the vitally important domain of student assessment "must center not on *how [they] assess* student achievement but on *how [they] use assessment* in pursuit of student success."[1] This chapter focuses on the following questions surrounding teachers' assessment of student learning:

♦ What does *assessment for learning* mean?

♦ What does the research say about *assessment for learning*?

♦ What are research-based quality indicators for *assessment for learning*?

♦ How can *assessment for learning* be documented?

♦ What are rating scale options for *assessment for learning*?

What Does *Assessment for Learning* Mean?

Gronlund described assessment as "a broad category that includes all of the various methods for determining the extent to which students are achieving the intended learning outcomes of instruction."[2] Assessment of student learning can emerge in various formats, such as teacher observation, oral questioning, journal entries, portfolio entries, exit cards, skill inventories, homework assignments, project products, student opinions, interest surveys, criterion-referenced tests, or norm-based tests. Ultimately, assessment can facilitate instruction and learning in several ways, including those noted in Figure 5.1.

Figure 5.1. Key Influences of Assessment for Learning

How Assessment Impacts Teaching and Learning

♦ Provides diagnostic information regarding students' mental readiness for learning new content.

♦ Provides formative and summative information needed to monitor student progress and adjust instruction.

♦ Helps keep students motivated.

♦ Holds students accountable for their own learning.

♦ Provides opportunities to reexpose students to content.

♦ Helps students to retain and transfer what they have learned.[3]

Although teachers are engaged with assessment techniques that are increasingly sophisticated, it is essential to acknowledge that neither standardized tests nor classroom assessments are just *of* learning, but more importantly, *for* learning.[4]

Figure 5.2 provides a sample definition for the *Assessment for Learning* performance standard. The definitions can be used to help operationalize this teacher performance standard, *Assessment for Learning*.

Figure 5.2. Sample Definition for the Assessment for Learning Performance Standard

The teacher gathers, analyzes, and uses data, including state and district assessment data, to measure learner progress, guide instruction, and provide timely feedback.

What Does the Research Say About Assessment for Learning?

High-quality assessment can produce valid information about students' learning outcomes and provide insight into the effectiveness of teachers' instruction. Research indicates that teachers who introduce formative assessment into their classroom practice can effect substantial achievement gains. In their 1998 research review, Black and Wiliam examined a multitude of empirical studies to determine whether improvement in classroom assessments can lead to improvement in learning.[5] They found that formative assessment has substantial positive effects on student achievement, with effect size ranging from 0.3 to 0.7 standard deviations. In particular, they found that formative assessment is more effective for low achievers than for other students, thus, reducing an achievement gap while raising achievement overall at the same time.[6]

Assessments are more likely to have a positive influence on student learning when they exhibit the characteristics noted in Figure 5.3.

Figure 5.3. Assessment Characteristics that Positively Influence Student Learning

Assessment

♦ aligned with the framework of learning targets and instruction;

♦ of sufficient validity and reliability to produce an accurate representation of student learning;

♦ accompanied with frequent informative feedback, rather than infrequent judgmental feedback;

♦ involving students deeply in classroom review and monitoring;

♦ processes and results timely and effectively communicated; and

♦ documented through proper record keeping of learning results.[7]

Students as well as teachers have strong beliefs about the importance of feedback. Students report that informative feedback makes them aware of their mistakes, highlights ways to make corrections, and informs them of teacher expectations. Teachers report that providing feedback can be arduous and painstaking, but also they feel that it is an important part of instruction.[8]

As noted earlier, there are multiple methods for assessing student learning. Guskey found that teachers and administrators believed student portfolios were the most important type of assessment tool used to measure student learning, while district, state, and national assessments ranked the lowest.[9] Interestingly, homework ranked in the middle of Guskey's analysis of assessment types. Regardless of the type of assessment used, the more important issue is the practical value of the assessment in use. Tomlinson suggested that teachers must find a proper fit between students and the method being used to assess their learning.[10] Assessment, she posited, is a form of communication. Teachers must allow students to communicate their learning in a manner best suited to their needs.

Given the prevalence of standardized assessments at the state, regional, and national levels, both in the United States and in numerous countries around the globe, a brief comment on this particular type of assessment seems in order. The extant literature has documented both positive and negative impacts of standardized assessments on teachers' instruction and assessment at the classroom level. The positive evidence indicates that standardized tests motivate teachers to:

♦ Align their instruction to standards;

♦ Maximize instructional time;

♦ Work harder to cover more material in a given amount of instructional time; and

♦ Adopt a better curriculum or more effective pedagogical methods.[11]

Other research, however, reveals that high-stakes assessments force teachers to:

♦ Narrow the curriculum;

♦ Focus on memorization, drills, and worksheets;

♦ Allocate less time to higher-order skills; and

♦ Restrict their teaching to formulated approaches of instruction.[12]

Standardized assessment is not primarily concerned with what is going on in the daily classroom. Consequently, teachers should maintain a balance between state/national level assessments and classroom level assessments to optimize student learning.

What Are Research-Based Quality Indicators for Assessment for Learning?

As indicated in Chapter 1, quality indicators are used to do just what the term implies—*indicate*, in observable behaviors, the types and quality of performance associated with a given performance standard, in this instance, the *Assessment for Learning* performance standard. Quality indicators are tangible behaviors that can be observed or documented to determine the degree to which a teacher is fulfilling the *Assessment for Learning* performance standard.

Although the set of eight performance standards in the book is provided as a comprehensive description of a teacher's key responsibilities, the quality indicators that rest underneath a given performance standard are merely *examples*. Figures 5.4 and 5.5 are two sample lists of quality indicators for the *Assessment for Learning* performance standard, but bear in mind that the quality indicators selected for the lists are only examples.

Figure 5.4. Sample 1 of Quality Indicators for Assessment for Learning

The teacher

- uses preassessment data to develop expectations for students and for documenting learning.

- assesses student performance based on instructional standards and provides timely and specific feedback.

- uses a variety of formal and informal assessment strategies throughout instruction.

- collects and maintains a record of sufficient assessment data to support accurate reporting of student progress.

- develops tools and guidelines that help students assess, monitor, and reflect on their own work.

- reteaches material and/or accelerates instruction based on assessment to pace instruction appropriately for student interest and learning.

Figure 5.5. Sample 2 of Quality Indicators for Assessment for Learning

The teacher

- effectively addresses appropriate curriculum standards.

- uses assessment data, including those from state and local assessments, to design instruction that meets students' current needs and documents students' learning.

- uses a variety of formal and informal assessment strategies to guide and adjust instruction for remediation and as well as enrichment.

- measures and documents learner growth with informal and formal state and local assessments, as appropriate.

- provides ongoing, timely, and specific feedback.

- helps students assess, monitor, and reflect on their work.

- collects and maintains a record of sufficient assessment data to support accurate reporting of student progress.
- keeps an official record (e.g., grade book) of student learning.

How Can Assessment for Learning Be Documented?

The *Assessment for Learning* performance standard and related quality indicators describe *what is expected* of a teacher for quality work. It isn't enough, however, to know what is expected; we also must know *how to document* that the work is being done.

Historically, teacher work has been documented primarily, if not exclusively, through classroom observation. Observation does play an important role for documenting teachers' work for most performance standards, but is not the exclusive method. As Figure 2.5 indicates, both observation and portfolios/data logs are highlighted as valued information sources for accurately documenting the *Assessment for Learning* performance standard.[*]

Figure 5.6. Aligning Data Sources with the Assessment for Learning Standard

Performance Standard	Observation	Portfolio/ Data Log	Other Data Sources
Assessment for Learning	S	P	TBD

Note: P = primary data source; S = secondary data source; TBD = to be determined.

In the case of assessment for learning, portfolios/data logs tend to serve as a primary data source and observations as a secondary data source. Figure 5.7 is an abbreviated observation sample form and Figure 5.8 is a set of possible artifacts for inclusion in a portfolio/data log.

---

[*] Additional information sources (i.e., student surveys, measures of student progress) are detailed in other books recommended in the "Want to Know More" section in Part II of the book.

Figure 5.7. Sample Classroom Observation Form for Assessment for Learning

Classroom Observation Form*

Teacher: _____ School:_____

Date:_____ Time:_____

Contract Status: ☐ Induction ☐ Continuing

Pre-Conference held ☐ No ☐ Yes, date _____

Type of Observation ☐ Formal ☐ Informal ☐ Walkthrough

Observer _____

This observation form focuses on established teacher performance. A copy of the completed observation form is to be given to the teacher.

Standard 4: *Assessment for Learning*	SPECIFIC EXAMPLES:
Quality Indicators ♦ Informal and formal assessment ♦ Timely and specific feedback ♦ Assessment records ♦ Analyzes and interprets data ♦ Data-guided decisions	

* This is an abbreviated version of a comprehensive classroom observation form provided in Part II of the book. For illustration purposes, the selected quality indicators may vary from those provided in the chapter.

Figure 5.8. Suggested Set of Artifacts to Include in a Portfolio/Data Log for Assessment for Learning

Assessment for Learning Artifacts

♦ Brief report describing your record-keeping system and how it is used to monitor student progress.

♦ Copy of teacher-made tests and other assessment measures.

♦ Copy of scoring rubric used for evaluating a student project.

♦ Summary explaining grading procedures.

♦ Photocopies or photographs of student work with written comments.

- Samples of educational reports, progress reports, or letters prepared for parents or students.

- Copy of tables of specifications developed to align classroom assessment with intended learning outcomes and instruction.

- Copy of disaggregated analysis of student achievement scores on standardized tests.

- Copy of learning contracts developed by students.

- Copy of student journals of self-reflection and self-monitoring.

- Modified lesson plans or intervention plans that incorporated in which adjustments are made based on student assessment results.

What Are Rating Scale Options for Assessment for Learning?

As noted in Chapter 1, rating scales are used to determine the effectiveness of performance (i.e., "meets standard," "does not meet standard"). However, rating scales, alone, are too prone to subjectivity. A solution to this limitation of rating scales is to design and consistently apply a performance appraisal rubric to the judgment of *how well* the performance standard has been fulfilled.

Figures 5.9, 5.10 (page 62), and 5.11 (page 63) provide field-tested performance appraisal rubrics for the *Assessment for Learning* performance standard. Full sets of rubrics are provided in Part II of the book.

Figure 5.9. Three-Point Performance Rubric for Assessment for Learning

Proficient*	Needs Improvement	Unsatisfactory
The teacher systematically gathers, analyzes, and uses data to measure student progress, guide instruction, and provide timely feedback.	The teacher inconsistently uses a variety of assessment strategies, links assessment to intended learning outcomes, modifies instruction based on assessment data, and/or reports student progress in a timely fashion.	The teacher rarely conducts assessments, uses a range of assessment formats, and/or applies assessment data to the instructional decision-making process.

* "Proficient" is the baseline of acceptable performance for teachers and is the actual performance standard.

Figure 5.10. Four-Point Performance Rubric for Assessment for Learning

Exemplary *In addition to meeting the standard...*	Proficient*	Needs Improvement	Unsatisfactory
The teacher uses a variety of informal and formal assessments based on intended learning outcomes to assess student learning and teaches students how to monitor their own academic progress.	The teacher systematically gathers, analyzes, and uses data to measure student progress, guide instruction, and provide timely feedback.	The teacher uses a limited selection of assessment strategies, inconsistently link assessment to intended learning outcomes, and/or does not use assessment to plan/modify instruction.	The teacher uses an inadequate variety of assessment sources, assesses infrequently, does not use baseline or feedback data to make instructional decisions, and/or does not report on student progress in a timely manner.

* "Proficient" is the baseline of acceptable performance for teachers and is the actual performance standard.

Figure 5.11. Five-Point Performance Rubric for Assessment for Learning

Exemplary *The professional's work is exceptional. In addition to meeting the standard...*	Superior *In addition to meeting the standard...*	Proficient *The description is the actual performance standard.*	Developing/Needs Improvement	Unsatisfactory
The teacher consistently demonstrates expertise in using a variety of formal and informal assessments based on intended learning outcomes to assess learning. Also teaches learners how to monitor and reflect on their own academic progress.	The teacher often uses a variety of formal and informal assessments based on intended learning outcomes to assess student learning and teach learners to monitor their own academic progress.	The teacher gathers, analyzes, and uses data, including state assessment data, to measure learner progress, guide instruction, and provide timely feedback.	The teacher attempts to use a selection of assessment strategies to link assessment to learning outcomes, or uses assessment to plan/modify instruction, but is often ineffective.	The teacher consistently does not use baseline or feedback data to make instructional decisions and does not report on learner progress in a timely manner.

Notes

1   Stiggins, R. J. (1999).

2   Gronlund, N. E. (2006).

3   Gronlund, N. E. (2006).

4   Stiggins, R. J. (2002).

5   Black, P. J., & Wiliam, D. (1998).

6   Black, P. J., & Wiliam, D. (1998).

7   Black, P. J., & Wiliam, D. (1998); Stiggins, R., & DuFour, R. (2009).

8   Zacharias, N. T. (2007).

9   Guskey, T. R. (2007).

10   Tomlinson, C. A. (2007).

11   Borko, H., & Elliott, R. (1999); Shepard, L. A., & Dougherty, K. C. (1991); Thayer, Y. (2000); Vogler, K. E. (2002).

12   Hamilton, L., & Stecher, B. (2004); Jones, B. D., & Egley, R. J. (2004); Jones, G., Jones, B. D., Hardin, B., Chapman, L., Yardrough, T., & Davis, M. (1999); Stecher, B. M., & Mitchell, K. J. (1995).

6

Learning Environment

Students need an engaging, stimulating, and enriching learning environment to grow and thrive. To achieve this type of rich environment, effective teachers establish and communicate guidelines for expected behavior, monitor student behavior, keep students on tasks, and infuse humor, care, and respect into the classroom interactions so as to develop a climate that is conducive to student learning. As a result, research indicates that a positive learning environment can shape student outcomes in cognitive, motivational, emotional, and behavioral domains.[1] This chapter explores the following questions related to creating and sustaining positive, robust learning environments:

- What does *learning environment* mean?
- What does the research say about *learning environment*?
- What are research-based quality indicators for *learning environment*?
- How can *learning environment* be documented?
- What are rating scale options for *learning environment*?

What Does *Learning Environment* Mean?

Caring, supportive, safe, challenging, academically robust—these attributes, among others, help define what it means to have a positive learning environment that is conducive to student success. However it is defined, virtually all teachers and administrators, and even students, themselves, recognize how valuable a positive classroom climate is to learning. The most prevalent criteria used to define learning environment are probably the physical arrangement of the classroom, discipline and routines, organization of learning activities, and the engagement of students with tasks, among others. These key features are highlighted in Figure 6.1 in an effort to elucidate the meaning of *learning environment*.

Figure 6.1. Key Characteristics of Learning Environment for Effective Teachers

Defining Characteristics of Positive Learning Environment	Focus
Physical arrangement of the classroom	The teacher develops functional floor plans with teacher and student work areas and furniture/materials placement for optimal benefit.[2]
Discipline and routines	The teacher establishes classroom rules and procedures early on in the school year.[3]
Organization of learning activities	Classroom activities have an academic focus. The teacher orchestrates smooth transitions and maintains momentum throughout teaching and learning.[4]
Engagement of students	The teacher uses effective questioning, smooth transition, and challenging but interesting activities to increase student engagement in learning and student accountability.[5]
Maximizing instructional time	The teacher protects instruction from disruption and makes the most out of every instructional moment.[6]
Communication of high expectations	The teacher assumes responsibility for student learning, sets high (but reasonable) expectations for all students, and supports students in achieving them.[7]
Care and respect	The teacher establishes rapport and trustworthiness with students by being fair, caring, respectful, and enthusiastic.[8]

Figure 6.2 provides two sample definitions for the *Learning Environment* performance standard. These definitions can be used to help operationalize the teacher performance standard, *Learning Environment*.

Figure 6.2. Sample Definitions for the Learning Environment Performance Standard

Sample 1: Learning Environment

The teacher uses resources, routines, and procedures to provide a positive, safe, student-centered environment that is academically challenging and respectful.

Sample 2: Learning Environment

The teacher creates and maintains a safe classroom environment while encouraging fairness, respect, and enthusiasm.

What Does the Research Say about Learning Environment?

Good teachers must be proficient in creating a positive classroom environment for learning, otherwise learning—at least the intended learning—will not occur. A review of research connecting learning environment and student achievement emphasizes a number of key dimensions, including classroom management and structure, positive classroom climate, and classroom talk.

Classroom Management and Structure

Teachers who emphasize structure in the classroom are more effective than those who do not.[9] In general, structure means "an aggregate of elements of an entity in their relationships to each other."[10] For our purposes in education, specifically, structure involves physically orienting the classroom for instruction, preparing and organizing materials, and framing lessons in a coherent and logical manner.

Effective teachers implement good classroom management to establish order, engage students, elicit student cooperation, with an ultimate purpose to establish and maintain an environment conducive to instruction and learning.[11] The extant research is fairly clear that good classroom management has a positive influence on students' motivational development.

A study conducted by one team of researchers found that students' perception of rule clarity and teacher monitoring are positively related to their development of academic interest in secondary school mathematics classes.[12] Another empirical study revealed that the top-quartile teachers (i.e., the most effective teachers as identified by the high academic achievement of the students they taught) were more organized with efficient routines and procedures for daily tasks, and they communicated higher behavioral expectations to students than ineffective teachers. The top teachers also were found to have less disruptive student behaviors (on average, once every two hours) than do the less effective teachers (on average, once every twelve minutes).[13] Another research team noted that teachers who spend more time establishing instructional routines at the beginning of the school year did not need to exert as much effort on similar tasks later in the year.[14] The investment in initial organizational strategies yielded significant gains in reading scores throughout the year. In comparison, achievement gains were lower among students whose teachers did not demonstrate similar organization skills.

Positive Classroom Climate*

Effective teachers build a classroom climate where error (i.e., risk taking) is welcomed, where student questioning is high, where engagement is the norm, and where students can gain reputations as effective learners.[15] Wang, Haertel, and Walberg analyzed a knowledge base representing 11,000 statistical findings about student achievement in order to answer the question, "What helps students learn?"[16] They found classroom instruction and climate was the second most influential factor among six identified types of influence, second only to, but nearly as prominent as, student aptitude. Based

---

* This section is adapted from Robert Williams' unpublished paper. Mr. Williams is a doctoral student in Educational Policy, Planning, and Leadership, the College of William and Mary.

on this research synthesis, classroom climate refers to the sociopsychological dimensions of classroom life.[17]

Teachers who make the effort to engage in positive interactions with students make a difference in the academic and social development of their students. A constructive interaction with students is a motivator for students to act in accordance with the expectation of their teacher. Studies by Ladd and by Furrer and Skinner confirmed that low student achievement can result from stressful student–adult relationships, whereas positive relationships can lead to higher levels of student participation and engagement.[18] Teacher interactions with students have been found to have effects at all grade levels. Hamre and Pianta found that first-grade teachers who engaged in positive interactions with at-risk students reduced the probability of those students experiencing failure in the early grades.[19] Barney found that middle school students developed a more positive attitude toward course content when their teachers took the time to interact with them.[20] Pressley, Raphael, Gallagher, and DiBella demonstrated that secondary teachers who got to know their students personally were able to work with them to develop and achieve goals.[21]

Classroom Talk

The interaction between teacher and students, and among students, is another significant indicator of learning environment. Authority is more distributed than centralized through the communication that happens in a positive classroom environment. Additionally, the talk between teacher and student is personalized. Exemplary teachers have been found to use authentic conversation to learn about students and encourage students to engage their peer's ideas.[22]

Figure 6.3 summarizes the key features of these three attributes of the positive learning environment.

Figure 6.3. Summary of Selected Features of Positive Learning Environment

Positive Learning Environment Attributes	Features of Attributes
Classroom management and structure	◆ Identifying and communicating desirable behavior ◆ Consistently applying rules and procedures ◆ Monitoring student behavior ◆ Taking preventive rather than reactive management actions ◆ Pacing class activities and transiting between tasks smoothly ◆ Maximizing instructional time ◆ Keeping students on tasks ◆ Making learning meaningful[23]

Positive classroom climate	◆ Cooperation among teachers and students
	◆ Common interest and values
	◆ Pursuit of common goals
	◆ A clear academic focus
	◆ Well-organized and well-planned lessons
	◆ Explicit leaning objectives
	◆ Appropriate level of task difficulty for students
	◆ Appropriate instructional pace[24]
Classroom talk	◆ Respectful, supportive, and productive
	◆ Modeled by teachers
	◆ Practiced to students

What Are Research-Based Quality Indicators for Learning Environment?

As indicated in Chapter 1, quality indicators are used to do just what the term implies—*indicate*, in observable behaviors, the types and quality of performance associated with a given performance standard, in this instance, the *Learning Environment* performance standard. Quality indicators are tangible behaviors that can be observed or documented to determine the degree to which a teacher is fulfilling the *Learning Environment* performance standard.

Although the set of eight performance standards in the book is provided as a comprehensive description of a teacher's key responsibilities, the quality indicators that rest underneath a given performance standard are merely *examples*. Figures 6.4 and 6.5 are two sample lists of quality indicators for the *Learning Environment* performance standard, but bear in mind that the quality indicators selected for the lists are only examples.

Figure 6.4. Sample 1 of Quality Indicators for Learning Environment

The teacher

◆ promotes a climate of trust and teamwork within the classroom.

◆ respects and promotes the appreciation of diversity within the classroom.

◆ emphasizes continuous improvement toward student achievement.

◆ creates and maintains a physical setting that minimizes disruption and promotes learning and safety.

◆ establishes and maintains effective classroom rules and procedures communicating them to students and families.

◆ models caring, fairness, humor, courtesy, respect, active listening, and enthusiasm for learning.

◆ creates an attractive, warm, and supportive classroom environment.

Figure 6.5. Sample 2 of Quality Indicators for Learning Environment

The teacher

- establishes rapport, trust, and respect.

- creates and maintains a safe physical setting.

- models caring, fairness, courtesy, respect, active listening, and enthusiasm for learning.

- assists students in planning and organizing for assignments, long-range projects, and tests.

- recognizes and fosters appreciation of diversity and teamwork.

- engages students in the learning process.

- promotes respectful interactions that challenge and engage students within the learning environment.

- respects and promotes the appreciation of diversity.

- implements classroom and school rules, procedures, and routines in an effective, fair, and consistent manner.

- maximizes instructional time.

How Can Learning Environment Be Documented?

The *Learning Environment* performance standard and related quality indicators describe *what is expected* of a teacher for quality work. However, it isn't enough to know what is expected; we also must know *how to document* that the work is being done.

Historically, teacher work has been documented primarily, if not exclusively, through classroom observation. Observation does play an important role for documenting teachers' work for most performance standards, but is not the exclusive method. As Figure 6.6 indicates, both observation and portfolios/data logs are highlighted as valued information sources for accurately documenting the *Learning Environment* performance standard.[†]

Figure 6.6. Aligning Data Sources with the Learning Environment Standard

Performance Standard	Observa-tion	Portfolio/ Data Log	Other Data Sources
Learning Environment	P	S	TBD

Note: P = primary data source; S = secondary data source; TBD = to be determined.

[†] Additional information sources (i.e., student surveys, measures of student progress) are detailed in other books recommended in the "Want to Know More" section in Part II of the book.

In the case of learning environment, observation tends to serve best as a primary means of documentation, with portfolios/data logs serving as a secondary data source. Figure 6.7 is an abbreviated observation sample form and Figure 6.8 is a set of possible artifacts for inclusion in a portfolio/data log.

Figure 6.7. Sample Classroom Observation Form for Learning Environment

Classroom Observation Form*

Teacher: _____ School:_____

Date:_____ Time:_____

Contract Status: ☐ Induction ☐ Continuing

Pre-Conference held ☐ No ☐ Yes, date _____

Type of Observation ☐ Formal ☐ Informal ☐ Walkthrough

Observer _____

This observation form focuses on established teacher performance. A copy of the completed observation form is to be given to the teacher.

Standard 5: *Learning Environment*	SPECIFIC EXAMPLES:
Quality Indicators ♦ Climate of trust and respect ♦ Diversity appreciation ♦ Safe and positive environ- ment ♦ Time use ♦ Classroom rules/routines ♦ Student engagement	

* This is an abbreviated version of a comprehensive classroom observation form provided in Part II of the book. For illustration purposes, the selected quality indicators may vary from those provided in the chapter.

Figure 6.8. Suggested Set of Artifacts to Include in a Portfolio/Data Log for Learning Environment

Learning Environment Artifacts

♦ Student survey summary information (i.e., student surveys of teacher effectiveness or learning climate).

♦ List of classroom rules with a brief explanation of the procedures used to develop and reinforce them.

♦ Diagram of the classroom with identifying comments.

- Diagram of alternative classroom arrangements used for special purposes with explanatory comments.

- Schedule of daily classroom routines.

- Explanation of behavior management philosophy and procedures.

- Photocopy of classroom physical layout.

What Are Rating Scale Options for Learning Environment?

As noted in Chapter 1, rating scales are used to determine the effectiveness of performance (i.e., "meets standard," "does not meet standard"). However, rating scales, alone, are too prone to subjectivity. A solution to this limitation of rating scales is to design and consistently apply a performance appraisal rubric to the judgment of *how well* the performance standard has been fulfilled.

Figures 6.9, 6.10, and 6.11 provide field-tested performance appraisal rubrics for the *Learning Environment* performance standard. Full sets of rubrics are provided in Part II of the book.

Figure 6.9. Three-Point Performance Rubric for Learning Environment

Proficient*	Needs Improvement	Unsatisfactory
The teacher uses resources, routines, and procedures to provide a positive, safe, student-centered environment that is academically challenging and respectful.	The teacher inconsistently demonstrates expectations for student behavior and/or achievement.	The teacher rarely maintains acceptable expectations for student behavior and/or academic achievement.

* "Proficient" is the baseline of acceptable performance for teachers and is the actual performance standard.

Figure 6.10. Four-Point Performance Rubric for Learning Environment

Exemplary *In addition to meeting the standard…*	Proficient*	Needs Improvement	Unsatisfactory
The teacher consistently uses effective management strategies so that learning time is maximized and disruptions are minimized.	The teacher provides a well-managed, safe, student-centered environment that is academically challenging and respectful.	The teacher inconsistently addresses student behavior and needs required for a safe, positive social and academic environment.	The teacher inadequately addresses student behavior, displays a poor attitude with students, and/or ignores safety standards.

* "Proficient" is the baseline of acceptable performance for teachers and is the actual performance standard.

Figure 6.11. Five-Point Performance Rubric for Learning Environment

Exemplary *The professional's work is exceptional. In addition to meeting the standard...*	Superior *In addition to meeting the standard...*	Proficient *The description is the actual performance standard.*	Developing/Needs Improvement	Unsatisfactory
The teacher consistently provides a well-managed, safe, student-centered environment that is academically challenging and respectful.	The teacher often uses effective management strategies so that learning time is maximized and disruptions are minimized.	The teacher creates and maintains a safe classroom environment while encouraging fairness, respect, and enthusiasm.	The teacher attempts to address student behavior and needs required for a safe, positive, social, and academic environment, but is often ineffective.	The teacher consistently addresses student behavior in an ineffective manner or does not maintain a safe, equitable learning environment.

Notes

1 Ludtke, O., Robitzsch, A., Trautwein, U., & Kunter, M. (2009); Fraser, B. J., & Fisher, D. L. (1982).

2 Stronge, J. H. (2007).

3 Emmer, E. T., Evertson, C. M., & Worsham, M. E. (2003).

4 Marzano, R. J., Marzano, R. J., & Pickering, D. J. (2003).

5 Wang, M. C., Haertel, G. D., & Walberg, H. J. (1994).

6 Good, T. L., & Brophy, J. E. (1997); Cruickshank, D. R., & Haefele, D. (2001).

7 Corbett, D., Wilson, B., & Williams, B. (2002); Johnson, B. L. (1997).

8 Carter, P. J. (2003); Walls, R. T., Nardi, A. H., von Minden, A. M., & Hoffman, N. (2002).

9 Cameron, C. E., Connor, C. M., Morrison, F. J., Jewkes, A. M. (2008); Stronge, J. H. (2007); Zahorik, J., Halbach, A., Ehrle, K., & Molnar, A. (2003).

10 Merriam-Webster, Inc. (2006). p. 1828.

11 Emmer, E. T., & Stough, L. M. (2001).

12 Kunter, M., Baumert, J., & Koller, P. (2007).

13 Stronge, J. H., Ward, T. J., Tucker, P. D., & Hindman, J. L. (2008).

14 Cameron, C. E., Connor, C. M., Morrison, F. J., Jewkes, A. M. (2008).

15 Hattie, J. (2003).

16 Wang, M. C., Haertel, G. D., & Walberg, H. J. (1994).

17 Wang, M. C., Haertel, G. D., & Walberg, H. J. (1994). p. 76.

18 Cited in Hamre, B. K., & Pianta, R. C. (2005).

19 Hamre, B. K., & Pianta, R. C. (2005).

20 Barney, D. (2005).

21 Pressley, M., Rapael, L. Gallagher, J. D., & DiBella, J. (2004).

22 Allington, R. L., & Johnston, P. H. (2000).

23 Emmer, E. T., & Stough, L. M. (2001).

24 Wang, M. C., Haertel, G. D., & Walberg, H. J. (1994). p. 76.

7

Communication and Advocacy

The ability to communicate and collaborate on both a small- and a large-scale is one of the essential requisites for teacher effectiveness.[1] In fact, at the very core of effective teaching is effective communication. After all, teaching is communicating and, to a large extent, advocating for learners. This chapter addresses the following questions regarding communication and advocacy:

♦ What does *communication and advocacy* mean?

♦ What does the research say about *communication and advocacy*?

♦ What are research-based quality indicators for *communication and advocacy*?

♦ How can *communication and advocacy* be documented?

♦ What are rating scale options for *communication and advocacy*?

What Does *Communication and Advocacy* Mean?

Ultimately, the ability to help students understand facts and concepts, develop and apply new skills, and critique and reconstruct meaning in the world around them is what teaching is all about. And how do teachers achieve this extraordinary transfer of learning with their students? Through communication. Indeed, effective teaching cannot exist without effective communication.

A factor closely related to effective communication is effective advocacy for learners. Educating a child cannot be one person's work. Certainly, teachers must be responsible and accountable for what is under their control—the academic and nonacademic interactions with their students. Beyond this traditional responsibility, however, good teachers know they must reach beyond the walls of the classroom to solicit collaboration and support from school colleagues on behalf of their students. Furthermore, they understand the need to reach beyond the schoolhouse door to communicate and gain cooperation with families and others in a larger community of learners.[2]

Effective communication and advocacy empower teachers to reconceptualize themselves as change agents and advocates for their students. Figure 7.1 summarizes the defining characteristics associated with the important roles of communicator and advocate.

Figure 7.1. Key Characteristics of Communication and Advocacy for Effective Teachers

Communication and Advocacy	Defining Characteristics
Communication skills	Ability to ♦ package and deliver content meaningfully. ♦ create an engaging class culture. ♦ be sensitive to individual student needs. ♦ connect with the student, first, as a person and, then, as a learner.[3]
Advocacy for students	Ability to ♦ be an advocate of better strategies for meeting students' learning needs, by being an active learner who seeks, applies, and communicates professional knowledge of curriculum, instruction, assessment, and student development. ♦ be an advocate of teaching as a profession by appreciating and practicing principles, ethics, and legal responsibilities. ♦ be an advocate for the well-being of the whole educational organization by initiating, valuing, and maintaining collaboration and partnerships with various stakeholders.[4]

Figure 7.2 provides two sample definitions for the *Communication and Advocacy* performance standard. These definitions can be used to help operationalize the teacher performance standard, *Communication and Advocacy*.

Figure 7.2. Sample Definitions for the Communication and Advocacy Performance Standard

Sample 1. Communication

The teacher communicates effectively with students, school personnel, families, and the community.

Sample 2: Communication and Advocacy

The teacher communicates effectively with students, school personnel, families, and the community to enhance, promote, and advocate for student learning.

What Does the Research Say about Communication and Advocacy?

Effective teaching does not just entail knowledge, but also requires teachers to actualize interpersonal communication skills as they translate knowledge into meaningful student learning. Until one can get on a communication level with five-year-olds or thirteen-year-olds, one cannot be a teacher—at least, not a teacher that positively impacts student learning.

Effective Communication

Extant research provides evidence that students taught by teachers with greater verbal ability learn more than those taught by teachers with lower verbal ability.[5] Teachers with high verbal skills are perceived to be more capable of conveying ideas effectively and communicating with students in a compelling manner. Closely connected to this notion is the concept of "instructional communication competence," which has been studied widely in educational research. Instructional communication competence was defined by Cornett-DeVito and Worley as:

> [T]he teacher-instructor's motivation, knowledge, and skill to select, enact and evaluate effective and appropriate, verbal and nonverbal, interpersonal and instructional messages filtered by student-learners' perceptions, resulting in cognitive, affective and behavioral student-learner development and reciprocal feedback.[6]

One research team identified, interviewed, and observed eleven award-winning teachers to develop a better understanding of their instructional communication practices.[7] Their findings included the following themes related to communication practices in the classroom:

♦ *Understand the ebb and flow of the classroom*—The teachers used instructional objectives to plan effective classroom activities effectively, but they were not restrained by predefined plans. They adapted to the flow of the class and allowed for spontaneity. Additionally, they used effective communication to orient students to learning and help them integrate new information with previously learned information.

♦ *Use a wide repertoire of communication skills*—The teachers used a variety of communication behaviors, such as immediacy, humor, and clarity to sustain a positive and interactive environment.

♦ *Create relationships with students*—The teachers communicated with students about shared experiences to establish interpersonal rapport, and they communicated in an approachable manner through proxemics, kinetics, knowing first names, and so forth. They also encouraged an open, warm, and communicative environment that invited students' comments, questions, and responses.

Effective Advocacy

Effective teachers not only communicate competently with their students, but also they communicate actively with their professional peers to share best practice, seek advice and suggestions, and conduct collaborative inquires. Change is the constant theme in today's education, and teachers are increasingly challenged to keep abreast of innovations and new developments. They need to communicate with colleagues or others who possess needed information.[8]

Teachers who have a democratic vision about their profession act collaboratively and cooperatively with colleagues and other educational stakeholders. They no longer confine their responsibility to the particular classroom in which they teach; rather, they are committed to making a contribution to the students taught by other teachers, the school, the district, and the larger community.[9] Michael Fullan corroborated this vision by proposing that teacher preparation programs should enable each teacher to initiate, value, and practice collaboration and partnerships with students, colleagues, parents, community, government, and social and business agencies.[10] Additionally, teachers of democratic professionalism serve as advocates for the well-being of the educational cause. They act individually and collectively to effect social justice and equity in teaching and learning. They are engaged in purposeful and critical reflection and dialogues with others on issues that have immediate impact on day-to-day classroom teaching, as well as larger issues and contexts that have indirect influence on social equity in education.[11]

Figure 7.3 is a selection of research findings related to communication and advocacy.

Figure 7.3. Selected Research Findings Related to Communication and Advocacy

Communication and Advocacy Attributes of an Effective Teacher

- ◆ Possesses strong communication skills.[12]
- ◆ Offers clear explanations and directions.[13]
- ◆ Recognizes the levels of involvement ranging from networking to collaboration.[14]
- ◆ Uses multiple forms of communication between school and home.[15]
- ◆ Uses informal contacts at school events, the grocery store, and at other community places to keep the lines of communication open.[16]

What Are the Research-Based Quality Indicators for Communication and Advocacy?

As indicated in Chapter 1, quality indicators are used to do just what the term implies—*indicate*, in observable behaviors, the types and quality of performance associated with a given performance standard, in this instance, the *Communication and Advocacy* performance standard. Quality indicators are tangible behaviors that can be observed or documented to determine the degree to which a teacher is fulfilling the *Communication and Advocacy* performance standard.

Although the set of eight performance standards in the book is provided as a comprehensive description of a teacher's key responsibilities, the quality indicators that rest underneath a given performance standard are merely *examples*. Figures 7.4 and 7.5 are two sample lists of quality indicators for the *Communication and Advocacy* performance standard, but bear in mind that the quality indicators selected for the lists are only examples.

Figure 7.4. Sample 1 of Quality Indicators for Communication and Advocacy

The teacher

♦ uses precise language, correct vocabulary and grammar, and acceptable forms of oral and written expression.

♦ explains directions, concepts and lesson content to students in a logical, sequential, and age-appropriate manner.

♦ shares major instructional goals and classroom expectations with families.

♦ initiates communication and responds to families or guardians concerning student expectations, progress or problems in a timely and confidential manner.

♦ coordinates efforts with school staff, other service providers, and community resources to reach educational decisions that enhance student learning.

♦ supports, promotes, and communicates the strategic plan, policies, regulations, and school events.

♦ uses technology (e.g., e-mail) to support and enhance communication as appropriate.

♦ communicates appropriately with all stakeholders, such as students, colleagues, administrators, other school personnel, community members, and families.

Figure 7.5. Sample 2 of Quality Indicators for Communication and Advocacy

The teacher

♦ uses understandable language and acceptable forms of oral and written communication.

♦ initiates two-way and engaging communication.

♦ communicates with students and parents/guardians regarding student expectations, progress, or concern in a timely and confidential manner.

♦ responds to concerns and/or problems in a timely and constructive manner, maintaining confidentiality.

- demonstrates sensitivity to the social and cultural background of students, parent and others.

- models various effective communication strategies.

- adheres to school and district policies regarding communication of student information.

- collaborates with colleagues from other fields/content areas in the integration of instruction and/or services.

- supports, promotes, and communicates the mission, vision, and goals of the school and school district.

How Can Communication and Advocacy Be Documented?

The *Communication and Advocacy* performance standard and related quality indicators describe *what is expected* of a teacher for quality work. However, it isn't enough to know what is expected; we also must know *how to document* that the work is being done.

Historically, teacher work has been documented primarily, if not exclusively, through classroom observation. Observation does play an important role for documenting teachers' work for most performance standards, but is not the exclusive method. As Figure 7.6 indicates, both observation and portfolios/data logs are highlighted as valued information sources for accurately documenting the *Communication and Advocacy* performance standard.*

Figure 7.6. Aligning Data Sources with the Communication and Advocacy Standard

Performance Standard	Observation	Portfolio/Data Log	Other Data Sources
Communication and Advocacy	P	P	TBD

Note: P = primary data source; S = secondary data source; TBD = to be determined.

In the case of *Communication and Advocacy*, both observations and portfolios/data logs can serve as primary data sources. Figure 7.7 is an abbreviated observation sample form and Figure 7.8 is a set of possible artifacts for inclusion in a portfolio/data log.

---

* Additional information sources (i.e., student surveys, measures of student progress) are detailed in other books recommended in the "Want to Know More" section in Part II of the book.

Figure 7.7. Sample Classroom Observation Form for Professional Knowledge

Classroom Observation Form*

Teacher: _____ School:_____

Date:_____ Time:_____

Contract Status: ☐ Induction ☐ Continuing

Pre-Conference held ☐ No ☐ Yes, date _____

Type of Observation ☐ Formal ☐ Informal ☐ Walkthrough

Observer _____

This observation form focuses on established teacher performance. A copy of the completed observation form is to be given to the teacher.

Standard 6: *Communication and Advocacy*	SPECIFIC EXAMPLES:
Quality Indicators ♦ Precise use of language ♦ Logical, sequential, and developmentally appropriate explanations to students ♦ Goals and expectations communicated ♦ Positive interactions with parents/guardians, staff, and community members ♦ Appropriate outreach to community on behalf of students	

* This is an abbreviated version of a comprehensive classroom observation form provided in Part II of the book. For illustration purposes, the selected quality indicators may vary from those provided in the chapter.

Figure 7.8. Suggested Set of Artifacts to Include in a Portfolio/Data Log for Communication and Advocacy

Communication and Advocacy Artifacts

♦ Log of attempts to establish and maintain rapport through such measures as parent calls, personal notes, interventions, conferences, interest surveys, and extracurricular activities.

♦ Copy of classroom newsletters or other parent information documents.

- Agenda for open house or "back to school night" events.
- Copy of student newsletters or other student information documents.
- Field trip agenda.
- Copy of nonlinguistic presentation (e.g., handout, Power Point file) used in classroom instruction or in communication with other school personnel, parents, or other social/business agencies.
- Agenda and summary of outreaching and collaborative activities.

What Are Rating Scale Options for Communications and Community Relations?

As noted in Chapter 1, rating scales are used to determine the effectiveness of performance (i.e., "meets standard," "does not meet standard"). However, rating scales, alone, are too prone to subjectivity. A solution to this limitation of rating scales is to design and consistently apply a performance appraisal rubric to the judgment of *how well* the performance standard has been fulfilled.

Figures 7.9, 7.10, and 7.11 provide field-tested performance appraisal rubrics for the *Communication and Advocacy* performance standard. Note that full sets of rubrics are provided in Part II of the book.

Figure 7.9. Three-Point Performance Rubric for Communication and Advocacy

Proficient*	Needs Improvement	Unsatisfactory
The teacher communicates effectively with students, school personnel, families, and the community to enhance, promote, and advocate for student learning.	The teacher inconsistently communicates with students, staff, parents, or community in an effective manner and/or inconsistently communicates concepts and class expectations to students.	The teacher rarely communicates and responds to students, staff, parents, or community concerns and/or poorly articulates content and expectations to students.

* "Proficient" is the baseline of acceptable performance for teachers and is the actual performance standard.

Figure 7.10. Four-Point Performance Rubric for Communication and Advocacy

Exemplary In addition to meeting the standard…	Proficient*	Needs Improvement	Unsatisfactory
The teacher uses a variety of communication techniques to inform, network, and collaborate with others to enhance student learning.	The teacher communicates effectively with students, school personnel, families, and the community.	The teacher inconsistently or ineffectively communicates with others.	The teacher inadequately communicates with school community by poorly acknowledging concerns, responding to inquiries, and/or encouraging involvement with stakeholders.

* "Proficient" is the baseline of acceptable performance for teachers and is the actual performance standard.

Figure 7.11. Five-Point Performance Rubric for Communication and Advocacy

Exemplary The professional's work is exceptional. In addition to meeting the standard …	Superior In addition to meeting the standard …	Proficient The description is the actual performance standard.	Developing/Needs Improvement	Unsatisfactory
The teacher consistently uses a variety of communication techniques to inform, network, and collaborate with students, staff, and other members of the learning community to enhance student learning.	The teacher often communicates information and responds to students and other stakeholders in a highly effective manner.	The teacher communicates effectively with students, their parents or families, staff, and other members of the learning community.	The teacher often communicates with students, staff, and other members of the learning community in an inconsistent or ineffective manner.	The teacher consistently does not communicate effectively with students, staff and other members of the learning community.

Notes

1 Fullan, M. G. (1993).

2 Sachs, J. (2001).

3 Cornett-DeVito, M., & Worley, D. W. (2005). p. 315.

4 Fullan, M. G. (1993).

5 Rowan, B., Chiang, F. S., & Miller, R. J. (1997); Strauss, R. P., & Sawyer, E. A. (1986).

6 Cornett-DeVito, M., & Worley, D. W. (2005).

7 Worley, D., Tistworth, S., Worley, D. W., & Cornett-DeVito, M. (2007).

8 Catt, S., Miller, D., & Schallenkamp, K. (2007).

9 Sachs, J. (2001).

10 Fullan, M. G. (1993).

11 Peters, S., & Reid, D. K. (2009).

12 National Association of Secondary School Principals (NASSP). (1997); Peart, N. A. & Campbell, F. A. (1999).

13 Covino, E. A., & Iwanicki, E. (1996); Emmer, E. T., Evertson, C. M., & Anderson, L. M. (1980).

14 Rockwell, R. E., Andre, L. C., & Hawley, M. K. (1996).

15 Swap, S. A. (1993).

16 Collinson, V., Killeavy, M., & Stephenson, H. J. (1999).

8

Professionalism

Teacher professionalism encompasses key characteristics—professional competence, performance, and conduct—that reflect teachers' goals and purposes, capabilities, values and beliefs, and directly impact the effectiveness of teaching.[1] As a profession, teachers value and practice the principles, standards, ethics, and legal responsibilities of teaching.[2] And, as with any profession, they must be committed to and skilled in the areas of expertise that define teaching. This chapter focuses on professionalism within the context of the following questions:

- ◆ What does *professionalism* mean?
- ◆ What does the research say about *professionalism* of the teacher?
- ◆ What are research-based quality indicators for *professionalism*?
- ◆ How can *professionalism* be documented?
- ◆ What are rating scale options for *professionalism*?

What Does *Professionalism* Mean?

Professionalism, for the purposes of our discussion, might be considered to reflect three essential elements of any true profession:

1. Having and abiding by a set of professional and ethical standards of conduct;
2. Continuing development for the teacher; and
3. Contributing to the profession.

Figure 8.1 highlights key aspects of this broad-based definition of *professionalism*.

Figure 8.1. Key Areas of Professionalism for Effective Teachers

Professionalism Area	Focus[3]
Professional standards and ethics of the profession	♦ Adhere to legal and ethical guidelines ♦ Adhere to standards defined for the profession ♦ Demonstrate professional demeanor and positive interaction with others ♦ Respect the diversity of ethnicity, race, gender, and special needs
Continuous self professional development	♦ Act as reflective practitioner ♦ Acquire and refine professional knowledge and skill ♦ Engage in ongoing professional renewal ♦ Act, as appropriate, as risk taker, stepping out of comfort zone ♦ Embrace practices of a life-long learner
Contributions to the profession	♦ Serve as role model for other educators ♦ Serve on school, district, regional, and state educational committees, work groups, etc. ♦ Participate in professional associations ♦ Contribute to the development of the profession (e.g., through presentations, writing)

Figure 8.2 provides two sample definitions for the *Professionalism* performance standard. These definitions can be used to help operationalize the teacher performance standard, *Professionalism*.

Figure 8.2. Sample Definitions for the Professionalism Performance Standard

Sample 1. Professionalism

The teacher maintains a professional demeanor, participates in professional growth opportunities, and contributes to the profession.

Sample 2. Professionalism

The teacher maintains a commitment to professional ethics and the mission of the school. The teacher takes responsibility for and participates in professional growth that results in enhancement of student learning.

What Does the Research Say About Professionalism of the Teacher?

Professionalism and the Ethics of Teaching

Teachers' daily practice is grounded in the beliefs, values, and attitudes they hold toward the profession, the students, the schools, and themselves.[4] To illustrate, caring about students is one of most widely documented personal qualities of effective teachers. Good teachers are often described as warm, friendly, and caring; conversely, ineffective teachers often are said to create a tense classroom and are described as cold, abusive, and uncaring.[5] When students perceive that their teachers care about them, they respond by "optimizing their commitment to learning and putting forth greater efforts to reach their potential."[6]*

Additional examples of how teachers impact school success—and their own success—through their professional demeanor and ethical treatment of others might include a personal quality as simple as attitude. In particular, enthusiasm and motivation are two essential attitudes that impact on teacher effectiveness and, ultimately, student achievement. Even teachers' enthusiasm for the teaching profession has positive effects on their instructional behaviors.[7] Teachers who are more enthusiastic about teaching exhibit higher quality instructional behavior, such as monitoring student learning, providing students with more cognitive autonomy support, offering more social support to students, and using higher levels of cognitive challenge. Teacher motivation also is expressed in a range of teacher behaviors that are perceived to be conducive to student learning, such as enthusiasm in content area taught, interest about students' personal and developmental needs, participation in content-related activities outside of class time, and displaying value and emotion for students.[8]

Teachers who demonstrate care and concern toward their students are perceived more positively and are more effective in fact. And, as with the personal quality of caring, other qualities, such as fairness and respect, have a positive impact on the teacher's bearing and effectiveness within the school community. This ethic of care and, more broadly, an ethic of working within the context of ethical, legal, and professional standards of conduct, is a key component of professionalism.

Professionalism and Professional Growth

Another key attribute of professionalism is a commitment to continuous improvement and perpetual learning. Interestingly, effective teaches monitor and strengthen the connection between their own development and students' development.[9] Evidence indicates that teachers who receive substantial professional development can help students achieve more. For example, based on the findings of one meta-analysis, teachers who receive substantial professional development (in this instance, forty-nine hours) can boost their students' achievement about 21 percentile points, and this effect size is fairly consistent across content areas.[10]

---

* See Chapter 6 for a details regarding developing and maintaining a caring classroom environment.

Professionalism and Contributing to the Profession

Effective teachers act individually and collectively to advance the teaching profession, and act as shapers, promoters, and well-informed critics of educational policies, instructional innovations, and internal changes that impact on student learning.[11] A teacher can contribute to the teaching profession by engaging in various types of study, inquiry, and even experimentations to develop personal best practices. Individually, teachers are powerful resources to enrich the professional knowledge base about academic standards, curriculum, pedagogy, and assessment by reflecting and sharing personal "what works" and "what does not work." Collectively, teachers can network with professional associations and collaborate with social/business agencies to advance overall school improvement.

Figure 8.3 summarizes selected research findings regarding the importance of Professionalism for teacher effectiveness.

Figure 8.3. Teacher Effectiveness and Professional Behaviors and Dispositions

Selected Research Findings

Professional behaviors of effective teachers:

- Encourage linking professional growth goals to professional development opportunities.[12]

- Empower them to make changes to enhance learning experiences, resulting in better student retention, attendance, and academic success.[13]

- Emphasize selecting professional development offerings that relate to the content area or population of students taught, resulting in higher levels of student academic success.[14] For example, science teachers with professional development in laboratory skills have students who outperform their peers.

- Encourage cognizance of the legal issues associated with educational records, and respect and maintain confidentiality.[15]

What Are Research-Based Quality Indicators for Professionalism?

As indicated in Chapter 1, quality indicators are used to do just what the term implies—*indicate,* in observable behaviors, the types and quality of performance associated with a given performance standard, in this instance, the *Professionalism* performance standard. Quality indicators are tangible behaviors that can be observed or documented to determine the degree to which a teacher is fulfilling the *Professionalism* performance standard.

Although the set of eight performance standards in the book is provided as a comprehensive description of a teacher's key responsibilities, the quality indicators that rest underneath a given performance standard are merely *examples*. Figures 8.4 and 8.5 are two sample lists of quality indicators for the *Professionalism* performance standard, but bear in mind that the quality indicators selected for the lists are only examples.

Figure 8.4. Sample 1 of Quality Indicators for Professionalism

The teacher

- maintains a professional demeanor and behavior (e.g., appearance, punctuality, attendance).

- follows all applicable legal and procedural requirements (Family Education Rights and Privacy Act [FERPA], etc.).

- respects and maintains confidentiality and assumes responsibility for professional actions.

- handles administrative routines, policies, and procedures quickly and efficiently.

- represents the school/community favorably.

- evaluates and identifies areas of personal strength and weakness related to professional skills and their impact on student learning and sets goals for improvement of skills and professional performance.

- participates in professional growth activities (e.g., mentoring, peer coaching, and/or supervising practicing teachers or interns, attending conferences, participating in workshops, pursuing course work, and/or belonging to professional organizations at the district, state, and/or national level).

- serves on school and/or district committees and supports school activities.

Figure 8.5. Sample 2 of Quality Indicators for Professionalism

- Ethical Behavior

  The teacher

  - respects and maintains confidentiality.

  - maintains a positive pattern of professional behavior.

  - performs assigned duties.

  - follows policies and procedures.

- Professional Growth

  The teacher

  - evaluates and identifies areas of personal strengths and weaknesses related to professional skills and their impact on student learning.

  - sets goals for improvement of skills and professional performance.

  - incorporates learning from professional growth opportunities into instructional practice.

(Figure continues on next page.)

♦ Professional Contributions

The teacher

- serves on school and/or division committees.

- is an active participant in school improvement.

- works and contributes in a collaborative manner with the school community to enhance student learning.

How Can Professionalism Be Documented?

The *Professionalism* performance standard and related quality indicators describe *what is expected* of a teacher for quality work. However, it isn't enough to know what is expected; we also must know *how to document* that the work is being done.

Historically, teacher work has been documented primarily, if not exclusively, through classroom observation. Observation does play an important role for documenting teachers' work for most performance standards, but is not the exclusive method. As Figure 8.6 indicates, both observation and portfolios/data logs are highlighted as valued information sources for accurately documenting the *Professionalism* performance standard.[†]

Figure 8.6. Aligning Data Sources with the Professionalism Standard

Performance Standard	Observation	Portfolio/Data Log	Other Data Sources
Professionalism	P	P	TBD

Note: P = primary data source; S = secondary data source; TBD = to be determined.

In the case of the *Professionalism* performance standard, both observations and portfolios/data logs can serve as primary data sources. Figure 8.7 is an abbreviated observation sample form and Figure 8.8 (page 92) is a set of possible artifacts for inclusion in a portfolio/data log.

---

† Additional information sources (i.e., student surveys, measures of student progress) are detailed in other books recommended in the "Want to Know More" section in Part II of the book.

Figure 8.7. Sample Classroom Observation Form for Professionalism

Classroom Observation Form*

Teacher: _____ School:_____

Date:_____ Time:_____

Contract Status: ☐ Induction ☐ Continuing

Pre-Conference held ☐ No ☐ Yes, date _____

Type of Observation ☐ Formal ☐ Informal ☐ Walkthrough

Observer _____

This observation form focuses on established teacher performance. A copy of the completed observation form is to be given to the teacher.

Standard 7: *Professionalism*	SPECIFIC EXAMPLES:
Quality Indicators ♦ Professional ethics ♦ Professional demeanor ♦ Collaboration with school team ♦ Confidentiality ♦ School duties, policies, and procedures ♦ Reflection for professional growth ♦ Professional development ♦ Committee/school activity service	

* This is an abbreviated version of a comprehensive classroom observation form provided in Part II of the book. For illustration purposes, the selected quality indicators may vary from those provided in the chapter.

Figure 8.8. Suggested Set of Artifacts to Include in a Portfolio/Data Log for Professionalism

Professionalism Artifacts

- Resumé.
- Certificates from presentations given.
- Certificates from professional development activities attended (e.g., workshops).
- Thank you letter for serving as a mentor, cooperating teacher, and the like.
- Reflective journal professional development.
- Teacher log which documents professional thinking.
- Reflective journal entries about participating professional development activities.
- Samples of posting on professional webinars.

What Are Rating Scale Options for Professionalism?

As noted in Chapter 1, rating scales are used to determine the effectiveness of performance (i.e., "meets standard," "does not meet standard"). However, rating scales, alone, are too prone to subjectivity. A solution to this limitation of rating scales is to design and consistently apply a performance appraisal rubric to the judgment of *how well* the performance standard has been fulfilled.

Figures 8.9, 8.10, and 8.11 provide field-tested performance appraisal rubrics for the *Professionalism* performance standard. Full sets of rubrics are provided in Part II of the book.

Figure 8.9. Three-Point Performance Rubric for Professionalism

Proficient*	Needs Improvement	Unsatisfactory
The teacher maintains a commitment to professional ethics and the mission of the school. The teacher takes responsibility for and participates in professional growth that results in enhancement of student learning.	The teacher inconsistently demonstrates professional judgment, supports the school's mission, participates in professional growth activities, or applies strategies and information from professional growth opportunities.	The teacher demonstrates poor professional judgment, fails to support the school's mission, rarely takes advantage of professional growth opportunities, or fails to fulfill professional responsibilities.

* "Proficient" is the baseline of acceptable performance for teachers and is the actual performance standard.

Figure 8.10. Four-Point Performance Rubric for Professionalism

Exemplary *In addition to meeting the standard…*	Proficient*	Needs Improvement	Unsatisfactory
The teacher is a professional role model for others, engaging in a high level of personal professional growth, and contributes to the development of others and the well-being of the profession.	The teacher maintains a professional demeanor, participates in professional growth opportunities, and contributes to the profession.	The teacher inconsistently participates in professional growth activities, and opportunities to serve the profession, and/or displays lapses in professional judgment.	The teacher demonstrates inflexibility, a reluctance to support others in the work of the school, and rarely takes advantage of professional growth opportunities.

* "Proficient" is the baseline of acceptable performance for teachers and is the actual performance standard.

Figure 8.11. Five-Point Performance Rubric for Professionalism

Exemplary *The professional's work is exceptional. In addition to meeting the standard…*	Superior *In additional to meeting the standard…*	Proficient *The description is the actual performance standard.*	Developing/Needs Improvement	Unsatisfactory
The teacher at a high level consistently demonstrates professional conduct, contributes to the professional growth of others, and assumes a leadership role within the learning community.	The teacher demonstrates a high level of professional conduct, and often engages in a high level of professional growth, and contributes to the professional development of others.	The teacher demonstrates behavior consistent with legal, ethical, and professional standards and engages in continuous professional growth.	The teacher often does not display professional judgment or only occasionally participates in professional development activities.	The teacher does not adhere to legal, ethical, or professional standards, including all requirements for professional development activities.

Notes

1 *The role of teacher professionalism in education.* (n.d.).

2 Fullan, M. G. (1993).

3 Adapted from Fullan, M. G. (1993).

4 Vartuli, S. (2005).

5 Walls, R. T., Nardi, A. H., von Minden, A. M., & Hoffman, N. (2002).

6 Lumpkin, A. (2007).

7 Kunter, M., Tsiam Y., Klusmann, U., Brunner, M., Krauss, S., & Baumert, J. (2008).

8 Long, J. F., & Hoy, A. W. (2005).

9 Fullan, M. G. (1993).

10 Yoon, K. S., Duncan, T., Lee, S. W., Scarloss, B., & Shapley, K. L. (2007, December).

11 Little, J. W. (1993).

12 Danielson, C. (2001); Guskey, T. R. (2002).

13 ISTE research reports: Overview: Research on IT [informational technology] in education. (n.d.)

14 School Board News. (1997); Camphire, G. (2001).

15 Collinson, V., Killeavy, M., & Stephenson, H. J. (1999).

9

Student Progress

Both conventional wisdom and empirical research tell us that good teachers positively effect students' academic progress.[1] In fact, empirical research consistently has revealed that the teacher is the dominant school-related factor influencing academic growth.[2] This chapter addresses the following questions surrounding the topic of student progress:

♦ What does *student progress* mean?

♦ What does the research say about *student progress* and the teacher?

♦ What are research-based quality indicators for *student progress*?

♦ How can *student progress* be documented?

♦ What are rating scale options for *student progress*?

What Does *Student Progress* Mean?

Simply put, *Student Progress* means measurable student growth. Typically, student growth is operationally translated as academic growth, but it also can include a variety of legitimate avenues of school-related progress, such as in the areas of physical fitness and performing arts. Student growth in learning is the professional touchstone for the existence of educational programs and teaching. When we assess and document a teacher's performance or a school's worth, the academic gains of students taught must be taken into account—no matter what else is examined.[3]

Effective teachers not only positively impact student progress, but also they monitor student progress systematically and intelligently. And that is a commonly adopted strategy by effective teachers and an integral attribute of their instruction. That means student progress is not just the end, but also the means to reach the end by continuously monitoring success and step-by-step moving to desired learning outcomes. Student progress monitoring can be defined as the practice that helps teachers use student performance data to continuously evaluate the effectiveness of their teaching and make more informed instructional decisions.[4]

In an effort to more fully define what is meant by the performance standard, *Student Progress*, a few key features related to both impacting student progress as well as monitoring student progress are highlighted in Figure 9.1.

Figure 9.1. Key Attributes of the Performance Standard Student Progress

Student Progress Attributes	Features
Positively effecting student learning	◆ A teacher is effective in enabling students to grow academically across years, regardless of the students' socioeconomic status and prior achievement.[5] ◆ A teacher is able to produce higher-performing students than some current popular reform initiatives, such as class-size reduction, charter schools, school choice, and some other school-level structural reform.[6]
Actively monitoring student progress	◆ A teacher aligns intended learning outcomes, instruction, and assessment to effectively keep track of students' progress.[7] ◆ A teacher uses high-quality homework and classroom quizzes to review student performance on key knowledge and skills, and provide meaningful and timely feedback.[8] ◆ A teacher targets areas of strength and weakness to provide appropriate remediation.[9]

Figure 9.2 is a sample definition for the *Student Progress* performance standard. This definition can be used to help operationalize the teacher performance standard, *Student Progress*.

Figure 9.2. Sample Definitions for the Student Progress Performance Standard

Sample 1. Student Progress

The work of the teacher results in acceptable, measurable progress based on established standards.

What Does the Research Say About Student Progress of the Teacher?

A multitude of studies conducted in the United States and in other countries have documented the fact that effective teachers have a significant impact on student achievement. The research consistently has concluded that students in effective teachers' classrooms make academic growth that is larger than what's projected based on longitudinal data. Figure 9.3 summarizes selected key findings drawn from relevant empirical studies.

Figure 9.3. Summary Findings of the Relationship between Student Progress and Teacher Effectiveness

Key Findings

♦ Highly effective teachers were generally effective in helping all students progress, regardless of their prior achievement level, whereas ineffective teachers were found to be ineffective with all students. Average-effectiveness teachers facilitated achievement gains with lower-achieving students, but not higher-achieving students.[10]

♦ Teacher effects on student academic gains are cumulative and residual.[11]

♦ Variations in teacher quality account for at least 7.5 percent of the total variation in measured achievement gains.[12]

♦ Teachers contributed to 3 to 10 percent of the variability in student gain score, while controlling for student prior achievement and background characteristics.[13]

♦ Teachers who were highly effective in producing higher-than-expected student achievement gains (top quartile) in one end-of-course content test (reading, math, science, social studies) tended to produce top-quartile residual gain scores in all four content areas. Teachers who were ineffective (bottom quartile) in one content area tended to be ineffective in all four content areas.[14]

At a macro level, effective teachers help their students achieve more than what is predicted for them on summative, standardized assessments. At a micro level, effective teachers provide instruction and support that leads to quality learning opportunities on a day-to-day basis. For example, based on a large-scale research review, Hattie found that compared to their ineffective colleagues, effective teachers are adept at monitoring student problems and assessing their level of understanding and progress, and they provide much more relevant, useful feedback.[15] The research also shows that effective teachers are more adept at developing and testing hypotheses about learning difficulties or instructional strategies. Additionally, an experimental study reached the following conclusions for teachers who monitored their students' growth on a regular basis:

♦ They effected greater student achievement than those who used conventional monitoring methods.

♦ They had more improvement in their instructional structure.

♦ Their pedagogical decisions reflected greater realism and responsiveness to student progress.

♦ Their students were more knowledgeable of their own learning and more conscious of learning goals and progress.[16]

Student progress monitoring is a technique that can provide teachers with data on students' performance to evaluate the effectiveness of their instruction and make adjustments in their pedagogical behavior. Progress monitoring also can help teachers set meaningful student achievement goals to tap into greater student learning potential. Teachers who use progress monitoring also are better informed of the strengths and weaknesses in student learning and can better decide on what instructional modifications are necessary. Stecker, Fuchs, and Fuchs noted that teachers effected significant growth in student learning with progress monitoring only when they modified instruction based on progress monitoring data; however, frequent progress monitoring alone did not boost student achievement.[17]

What Are Research-Based Quality Indicators for Student Progress?

As indicated in Chapter 1, quality indicators are used to do just what the term implies—*indicate*, in observable behaviors, the types and quality of performance associated with a given performance standard, in this instance the *Student Progress* performance standard. Quality indicators are tangible behaviors that can be observed or documented to determine the degree to which a teacher is fulfilling the *Student Progress* performance standard.

Although the set of eight performance standards is provided as a comprehensive description of a teacher's key responsibilities, the quality indicators that rest underneath a given performance standard are merely *examples*. Figures 9.4 and 9.5 are two sample lists of quality indicators for the *Student Progress* performance standard, but bear in mind that the quality indicators selected for the lists are only examples.

Figure 9.4. Sample 1 of Quality Indicators for Student Progress

The teacher

♦ sets measurable and appropriate achievement goals for student progress.

♦ gathers and analyzes data on student academic achievement through standardized test results and other student performance sources.

♦ uses formative assessment to regularly monitor student progress and modify instruction as needed.

♦ provides evidence that achievement goals have been met.

♦ communicates/collaborates with colleagues in order to improve students' performance.

Figure 9.5. Sample 2 of Quality Indicators for Student Progress

The teacher

- demonstrates an understanding of the concepts, principles, and strategies that enable students to progress and be academically successful including the use of state and local assessments.

- establishes student achievement goals.

- provides evidence of goal attainment.

- collaborates with colleagues in order to improve students' performance.

- provides evidence of timely and appropriate intervention strategies for individual students not making adequate progress.

How Can Student Progress Be Documented?

The *Student Progress* performance standard and related quality indicators describe *what is expected* of a teacher for quality work. However, it isn't enough to know what is expected; we also must know *how to document* that the work is being done.

Historically, teacher work has been documented primarily, if not exclusively, through classroom observation. Observation does play an important role for documenting teachers' work for most performance standards, but is not the exclusive method. As Figure 9.6 indicates, both observation and portfolios/data logs are highlighted as valued information sources for accurately documenting the *Student Progress* performance standard.[*]

Figure 9.6. Aligning Data Sources with the Student Progress Standard

Performance Standard	Observation	Portfolio/Data Log	Other Data Sources
Student Progress	S	P	P

Note: P = primary data source, S = secondary data source; TBD = to be determined.

In the case of the *Student Progress* performance standard, portfolios/data logs can serve as a primary data source, whereas observation tends to serve as a secondary source. Additionally, "other data sources," specifically student achievement growth scores and other measures of student progress, can serve as a primary source. Documenting a teacher's success in terms of student progress virtually mandates the use of

---

[*] Additional information sources (i.e., student surveys, measures of student progress) are detailed in other books recommended in the "Want to Know More" section in Part II of the book.

actual measures of student growth and success; observing in a classroom, alone, simply will not suffice. Nonetheless, observation and reviewing relevant artifacts can help in better understanding what the achievement data report. Figure 9.7 is an abbreviated observation sample form and Figure 9.8 is a set of possible artifacts for inclusion in a portfolio/data log.

Figure 9.7. Sample Classroom Observation Form for Student Progress

Classroom Observation Form*

Teacher: _____ School:_____

Date:_____ Time:_____

Contract Status: ☐ Induction ☐ Continuing

Pre-Conference held ☐ No ☐ Yes, date _____

Type of Observation ☐ Formal   ☐ Informal   ☐ Walkthrough

Observer _____

This observation form focuses on established teacher performance. A copy of the completed observation form is to be given to the teacher.

Standard 8: *Student Progress* Quality Indicators ♦ Student progress goals set ♦ Goal monitoring ♦ Means of support identified and given to students ♦ Evidence of meeting achievement goals	SPECIFIC EXAMPLES:

* This is an abbreviated version of a comprehensive classroom observation form provided in Part II of the book. For illustration purposes, the selected quality indicators may vary from those provided in the chapter.

Figure 9.8. Suggested Set of Artifacts to Include in a Portfolio/Data Log for Student Progress

Student Progress Artifacts

- Performance Goal Setting Form
- Chart of student progress throughout the year
- Analysis of grades for the marking period
- Log of collegial collaboration
- Documentation of meeting established annual goals
- Test critique
- Table of key knowledge and skills that indicates level of student mastery
- Benchmarks chart to record student progress
- Teacher annual goals for improve student achievement
- Student profiles
- Annotated sample of homework assignments and feedback provided
- Copy of tables of specifications that align assessment with learning objectives and instruction
- Copy of disaggregated analysis of student achievement scores on standardized tests

What Are Rating Scale Options for Student Progress?

As noted in Chapter 1, rating scales are used to determine the effectiveness of performance (i.e., "meets standard," "does not meet standard"). However, rating scales, alone, are too prone to subjectivity. A solution to this limitation of rating scales is to design and consistently apply a performance appraisal rubric to the judgment of *how well* the performance standard has been fulfilled.

Figures 9.9, 9.10 (page 102), and 9.11 (page 102) provide field-tested performance appraisal rubrics for the *Student Progress* performance standard. Full sets of rubrics are provided in Part II of the book.

Figure 9.9. Three-Point Performance Rubric for Student Progress

Proficient*	Needs Improvement	Unsatisfactory
The work of the teacher results in acceptable, measurable student progress.	The work of the teacher inconsistently results in an acceptable level of student progress.	The work of the teacher rarely results in an acceptable level of student progress.

* "Proficient" is the baseline of acceptable performance for teachers and is the actual performance standard.

Figure 9.10. Four-Point Performance Rubric for Student Progress

Exemplary *In addition to meeting the standard…*	Proficient*	Needs Improvement	Unsatisfactory
The teacher attains a high level of student achievement with all populations of learners.	The work of the teacher results in acceptable, measurable progress based on established standards.	The work of the teacher results in student growth but does not meet the established standard and/or is not achieved with all populations taught by the teacher.	The work of the teacher does not achieve acceptable student growth.

* "Proficient" is the baseline of acceptable performance for teachers and is the actual performance standard.

Figure 9.11. Five-Point Performance Rubric for Student Progress

Exemplary *The professional's work is exceptional. In addition to meeting the standard…*	Superior *In addition to meeting the standard…*	Proficient *The description is the actual performance standard.*	Developing/Needs Improvement	Unsatisfactory
The teacher consistently takes a key leadership role in assisting other professionals to achieve high levels of learner progress, or the work of the teacher consistently results in recognition of high levels of learner progress or achievement.	The work of the teacher often results in a high level of student achievement and/or progress.	The work of the teacher results in acceptable and measurable learner progress based on established standards, district goals, and/or school goals.	The work of the teacher results in some student progress, but more progress is often needed to meet established standards, district goals, and/or school goals.	The work of the teacher consistently does not result in acceptable student progress.

Notes

1 Sanders, W. L, & Rivers, J. C. (1996, November); Nye, B., Konstantopoulos, S., & Hedges, L. V. (2004).

2 Sanders, W. L., & Rivers, J. C. (1996, November); Wright, S. P., Horn, S. P., & Sanders, W. L. (1997).

3 Schalock, H. D., & Schalick, M. D. (1993).

4 Safer, N., & Fleischman, S. (2005).

5 Schacter, J., & Thum, Y. M. (2004); Sanders, W. L., & Rivers, J. C. (1996, November).

6 Schacter, J., & Thum, Y. M. (2004).

7 Walker, M. H. (1998).

8 Danielson, C. (2002).

9 Tomlinson, C. A. (1999); Chappius, S., & Stiggins, R. J. (2002).

10 Aaronson, D., Barrow, L., & Sander, W. (2007); Sanders, W. L., & Rivers, J. C. (1996, November).

11 Sanders, W. L., & Rivers, J. C. (1996, November).

12 Hanushek, E. A., Kain, J. F., O'Brien, D. M., & Rivkin, S. G. (2005).

13 Rowan, B., Chiang, F. S., & Miller, R. J. (1997).

14 Stronge, J. H., Ward, T. J., Tucker, P. D., & Hindman, J. L. (2008).

15 Hattie, J. (2003).

16 Fuchs, L. S., Deno, S. L., & Mirkin, P. K. (1984).

17 Stecker, P. M., Fuchs, L. S., & Fuchs, D. (2005).

10

Concluding Thoughts on Evaluating Teacher Effectiveness

No educational reform or innovation can bring forth the intended changes in student learning unless those reforms and innovations make a dent in teacher effectiveness. Consistent with the belief that school improvement happens one classroom at a time, Ted Hershberg articulated quite well why we need to consider the teacher as the unit of analysis if we are to improve our schools:[1]

> NCLB [*No Child Left Behind*] moved in the right direction in requiring accountability. But in making the school rather than the individual educator the unit of accountability, it fell short for two important reasons. *First,* because there is greater variation in the quality of instruction *within* schools than *between* them, it is essential to report data at the classroom level for evaluation purposes. *Second,* systemic changes…will be achieved only when the career of everyone working in our public schools are tied to successful learning outcomes. (p. 279; emphasis added)

Why Evaluating Teacher Effectiveness Matters

Teachers' impact on student achievement is of such a magnitude that it has significant implications for policies and practices intended to improve school performance and educational productivity. Indeed, Mendro, Jordan, Gomez, Anderson, and Bembry proposed that the effects of teacher are on an order of magnitude which overwhelms the effects associated with curriculum, staff development, restructuring, and other types of educational interventions.[2] For example, consider class-size reduction, one of the most costly educational interventions. Research reveals that the contribution of class size to student achievement gains is less than one-twentieth of the contribution of teacher quality.[3] Correspondingly, a costly reduction in class size from twenty-five to fifteen has smaller effects than the benefits of moving teacher quality up one standard deviation.[4]

Because teachers are so fundamentally important to school improvement and student success, improving the evaluation of teacher performance is particularly relevant as a means to advance teacher effectiveness. An effective evaluation recognizes, appreciates, values, and develops good teaching. The benefits of an effective teacher evaluation system are numerous and well documented. Indeed, the process of teacher evaluation can be valuable in several ways, including:

♦ Assessing the effectiveness of classroom teachers;

♦ Identifying teachers' areas in need of improvement;

♦ Making professional development more individualized; and

♦ Improving instruction schoolwide.[5]

Why Evaluating Teacher Effectiveness is Challenging

In this time of increased accountability, it should be emphasized that teacher evaluation, if conducted correctly, can result in improved teacher performance and an increase in student achievement. However, in contrast to this ideal, the contemporary teacher performance evaluation systems used in most schools and school districts has little impact on teacher practice or student achievement. In fact, "the troubled state of teacher evaluation is a glaring, and largely ignored, problem in public education."[6]

The flaws, which include those identified in Figure 10.1, in the current teacher evaluation process are numerous.

Figure 10.1. Problems Associated with Contemporary Teacher Evaluation

♦ Problems with the evaluation instruments themselves (e.g., subjectivity, low validity)

♦ Issues related to time and resources[7]

♦ Tendency to focus on paperwork routines rather than improving instruction

♦ Absence of standard protocols and practices in teacher practices

♦ Absence of meaningful and timely feedback to teachers

♦ Inadequate administrator training

♦ Lack of time to perform adequate evaluations[8]

♦ Lack of impact

Additionally, teacher evaluations tend to be uncritical and based on sparse evidence.

As a consequence of the above-noted pervasive problems, teacher performance evaluation too often has deteriorated into a "superficial, capricious, and often meaningless exercise."[9] Unsurprisingly, teacher responses to evaluation include a lack of understanding that evaluation can be used as a means of improving their performance.[10]

Evaluating Teacher Effectiveness: How Can We Make a Difference?

As noted in the *Preface*, the primary purpose of *Evaluating What Good Teachers Do: Eight Research-based Standards for Assessing Teacher Effectiveness* is to help both teachers and their evaluators collect more comprehensive and accurate assessment data for judging teacher effectiveness. Each chapter presented details about how a given teacher performance quality can be documented. It is well-established that students learn best when taught by effective teachers, but it is difficult to know who these effective teachers are without a well-designed and well-implemented teacher assessment system.[11] *Evaluating What Good Teachers Do* examines key elements for constructing an effective and fair performance evaluation system for teachers. This book will be a useful tool to the frontline evaluators who work at assessing and supporting teacher quality. Moreover, our teachers can embrace and benefit from quality assessment of their important work—educating our children.

Notes

1 Hershberg, T. (2005).

2 Mendro, R. L., Jordan, H. R., Gomez, E., Anderson, M. C., & Bembry, K. L. (1998, April).

3 Hanushek, E. A., Kain, J. F., & Rivkin, S. G. (1998, August).

4 Rivkin, S. G., Hanushek, E. A., & Kain, J. F. (2005).

5 Johnston, D. L. (1999).

6 Cited in Keller, B. (2008, January 16). p. 8.

7 Heneman, H. G., & Milanowski, A. T. (2003).

8 Loup, K. S., Garland, J. S., Ellett, C. D., & Rugutt, J. K. (1996).

9 Cited in Keller, B. (2008). p. 8.

10 Frase, L. E., & Streshly, W. (1994); Heneman, H. G., & Milanowski, A. T. (2003).

11 Stronge, J. H. (2006).

Part II

Tools You Can Use

Teacher Performance Standards*

Performance Standard 1: Knowledge of Curriculum, Subject Content, and Developmental Needs

Definition

The teacher demonstrates an understanding of the curriculum, subject content, and the developmental needs of students by providing relevant learning experiences.

Sample Quality Indicators

The teacher

- effectively addresses appropriate curriculum standards.

- integrates key content elements and higher level thinking skills in instruction.

- demonstrates ability to link present content with past and future learning experiences, other subject areas, and real world experiences and applications.

- demonstrates accurate knowledge of subject matter.

- demonstrates skills relevant to the subject area(s) taught.

- bases instruction on goals that reflect high expectations, and understanding of the subject.

- understands intellectual, social, emotional, and physical development of the age group.

---

* All observation forms and performance appraisal rubrics used in the book are copyrighted to James H. Stronge. They were developed and field-tested with numerous school districts in the United States, and are used here with permission granted from the author.

Performance Appraisal Rubrics

Three-Point Performance Rubric for Professional Knowledge

Proficient*	Developing/Needs Improvement	Unsatisfactory
The teacher demonstrates an understanding of the curriculum, subject content, and the developmental needs of students.	The teacher inconsistently demonstrates understanding in the area(s) of curriculum, content, or student development; or inconsistently uses the knowledge for effective instruction.	The teacher bases instruction on information that is inaccurate or out-of-date and/or inadequately addresses the developmental needs of students.

* "Proficient" is the baseline of acceptable performance for teachers and is the actual performance standard.

Four-Point Performance Rubric for Professional Knowledge

Exemplary In addition to meeting the standard…	Proficient*	Developing/ Needs Improvement	Unsatisfactory
The teacher consistently demonstrates extensive knowledge of the subject matter and continually enriches the curriculum.	The teacher demonstrates an understanding of the curriculum, subject content, and the developmental needs of students by providing relevant learning experiences.	The teacher inconsistently demonstrates understanding of curriculum, content, and student development or lacks fluidity of using the knowledge in practice.	The teacher bases instruction on material that is inaccurate or out-of-date and/or inadequately addresses the developmental needs of students.

* "Proficient" is the baseline of acceptable performance for teachers and is the actual performance standard.

Five-Point Performance Rubric for Professional Knowledge

Exemplary	Superior	Proficient	Developing/ Needs Improvement	Unsatisfactory
The professional's work is exceptional. In addition to meeting the standard…	*In addition to meeting the standard…*	*The description is the actual performance standard.*		
The teacher consistently plays a leadership role by integrating knowledge of learners to address the needs of the target learning community.	The teacher often meets the individual and diverse needs of learners in a highly effective manner.	The teacher identifies and addresses the needs of learners by demonstrating respect for individual differences, cultures, backgrounds, and learning styles.	The teacher attempts, but is often ineffective in demonstrating knowledge and understanding of the needs of the target learning community.	The teacher consistently demonstrates a lack of awareness of the needs of the target learning community or does not consistently make appropriate accommodations to meet those needs.

Performance Standard 2: Data-Driven Planning

Definition

The teacher plans for the use of appropriate curricula, instructional strategies, and resources to address the needs of all students.

Sample Quality Indicators

The teacher

- ♦ develops plans that are clear, logical, sequential, and integrated across the curriculum (e.g., long-term goals, lesson plans, and syllabi).

- ♦ matches content/skills taught to overall curriculum scope and sequence.

- ♦ evaluates curricular materials for accuracy, currency, and student interest.

- ♦ designs coherent instruction based upon knowledge of subject matter, students, the community, and curriculum standards and goals.

- ♦ demonstrates the ability to evaluate and refine existing materials and to create new materials when necessary.

♦ identifies and plans for the instructional and developmental needs of all students, including remedial, high achievers, and identified gifted students.

Performance Appraisal Rubrics

Three-Point Performance Rubric for Data-Driven Planning

Proficient*	Needs Improvement	Unsatisfactory
The teacher plans for the use of appropriate curricula, instructional strategies and resources to address the needs of *all* students.	The teacher inconsistently uses appropriate curricula, instructional strategies, and resources during the planning process to address the needs of all students.	The teacher rarely appropriate curricula, instructional strategies, and resources during the planning process to address the needs of students.

* "Proficient" is the baseline of acceptable performance for teachers and is the actual performance standard.

Four-Point Performance Rubric for Data-Driven Planning

Exemplary *In addition to meeting the standard…*	Proficient*	Needs Improvement	Unsatisfactory
The teacher's planning process consistently anticipates student misconceptions and/or prior knowledge by employing a variety of instructional strategies and resources.	The teacher's planning uses appropriate curricula, instructional strategies, and resources to address the needs of all students.	The teacher's planning displays inconsistent use of curricula, strategies, and/or resources to meet students' needs.	The teacher's planning inadequately meets the needs of the learners and/or follows the adopted curriculum.

* "Proficient" is the baseline of acceptable performance for teachers and is the actual performance standard.

Five-Point Performance Rubric for Data-Driven Planning

Exemplary *The professional's work is exceptional. In addition to meeting the standard…*	Superior *In addition to meeting the standard…*	Proficient *The description is the actual performance standard.*	Developing/ Needs Improvement	Unsatisfactory
The teacher consistently creates standards-based curricula and evaluates appropriate curricula, instructional strategies, and resources to plan and modify instruction in order to address the diverse needs of students.	The teacher often uses appropriate curricula, instructional strategies, and resources to plan, modify, and adjust instruction in order to meet the diverse needs of students.	The teacher uses appropriate curricula, instructional strategies, and resources during the planning process, including state reading requirements, to address the diverse needs of students.	The teacher attempts to use appropriate curricula, instructional strategies, and/or resources during the planning process, but is often ineffective in meeting the diverse needs of all learners.	The teacher consistently demonstrates a lack of planning or does not properly address the curriculum in meeting the diverse needs of all learners.

Performance Standard 3: Instructional Delivery

Definition

The teacher promotes student learning by addressing individual learning differences and by using effective instructional strategies.

Sample Quality Indicators

The teacher

- ◆ modifies instruction to make topics relevant to students' lives and experiences.

- ◆ uses materials, technology, and resources to provide learning experiences that challenge, motivate, and actively involve the learner.

- ◆ uses a variety of appropriate teaching strategies, which may include grouping, cooperative, peer and project-based learning, audiovisual presentations, lecture, discussions and inquiry, practice and application, and questioning, etc.

♦ paces instruction appropriately with adequate preview and review of instructional components.

♦ solicits comments, questions, examples, and other contributions from students throughout lessons.

♦ demonstrates ability to engage and maintain students' attention and to recapture or refocus it as necessary.

Performance Appraisal Rubrics

Three-Point Performance Rubric for Instructional Delivery

Proficient*	Needs Improvement	Unsatisfactory
The teacher promotes student learning by addressing individual learning differences and by using effective instructional strategies.	The teacher inconsistently addresses individual learning differences and/or use effective instructional strategies.	The teacher rarely delivers effective instruction.

* "Proficient" is the baseline of acceptable performance for teachers and is the actual performance standard.

Four-Point Performance Rubric for Instructional Delivery

Exemplary *In addition to meeting the standard…*	Proficient*	Needs Improvement	Unsatisfactory
The teacher's instructional delivery optimizes students' opportunity to learn by engaging students in higher-order thinking skills and processes to address divergent learning needs.	The teacher promotes student learning by addressing individual learning differences and by using effective instructional strategies.	The teacher inconsistently differentiates instruction and/or uses limited instructional strategies.	The teacher offers instruction that inadequately addresses differences in students' learning needs.

* "Proficient" is the baseline of acceptable performance for teachers and is the actual performance standard.

Five-Point Performance Rubric for Instructional Delivery

Exemplary *The professional's work is exceptional. In addition to meeting the standard…*	Superior *In addition to meeting the standard…*	Proficient *The description is the actual performance standard.*	Developing/ Needs Improvement	Unsatisfactory
The teacher consistently optimizes learning by engaging all groups of students in higher-order thinking and by effectively implementing a variety of appropriate instructional strategies and technologies.	The teacher often promotes learning by addressing the academic needs of all groups of students at a high level, and by using a variety of appropriate instructional strategies and technologies.	The teacher promotes learning by demonstrating accurate content knowledge and by addressing academic needs through a variety of appropriate instructional strategies and technologies that engage learners.	The teacher attempts to use instructional strategies or technology to engage students, but is often ineffective or needs additional content knowledge.	The teacher lacks content knowledge or does not consistently implement instructional strategies to academically engage learners.

Performance Standard 4: Assessment for Learning

Definition

The teacher systematically gathers, analyzes, and uses data to measure student progress, guide instruction, and provide timely feedback.

Sample Quality Indicators

The teacher

- ♦ uses preassessment data to develop expectations for students and for documenting learning.

- ♦ assesses student performance based on instructional standards and provides timely and specific feedback.

- ♦ uses a variety of formal and informal assessment strategies throughout instruction.

- collects and maintains a record of sufficient assessment data to support accurate reporting of student progress.

- develops tools and guidelines that help students assess, monitor, and reflect on their own work.

- reteaches material and/or accelerates instruction based on assessment to pace instruction appropriately for student interest and learning.

Performance Appraisal Rubrics

Three-Point Performance Rubric for Assessment for Learning

Proficient*	Needs Improvement	Unsatisfactory
The teacher systematically gathers, analyzes, and uses data to measure student progress, guide instruction, and provide timely feedback.	The teacher inconsistently uses a variety of assessment strategies, links assessment to intended learning outcomes, modifies instruction based on assessment data, and/or reports student progress in a timely fashion.	The teacher rarely conducts assessments, uses a range of assessment formats, and/or applies assessment data to the instructional decision-making process.

* "Proficient" is the baseline of acceptable performance for teachers and is the actual performance standard.

Four-Point Performance Rubric for Assessment for Learning

Exemplary *In addition to meeting the standard…*	Proficient*	Needs Improvement	Unsatisfactory
The teacher uses a variety of informal and formal assessments based on intended learning outcomes to assess student learning and teaches students how to monitor their own academic progress.	The teacher systematically gathers, analyzes, and uses data to measure student progress, guide instruction, and provide timely feedback.	The teacher uses a limited selection of assessment strategies, inconsistently link assessment to intended learning outcomes, and/or does not use assessment to plan/modify instruction.	The teacher uses an inadequate variety of assessment sources, assesses infrequently, does not use baseline or feedback data to make instructional decisions, and/or does not report on student progress in a timely manner.

* "Proficient" is the baseline of acceptable performance for teachers and is the actual performance standard.

Five-Point Performance Rubric for Assessment for Learning

Exemplary	Superior	Proficient	Developing/ Needs Improvement	Unsatisfactory
The professional's work is exceptional. In addition to meeting the standard…	*In addition to meeting the standard…*	*The description is the actual performance standard.*		
The teacher consistently demonstrates expertise in using a variety of formal and informal assessments based on intended learning outcomes to assess learning. Also teaches learners how to monitor and reflect on their own academic progress.	The teacher often uses a variety of formal and informal assessments based on intended learning outcomes to assess student learning and teach learners to monitor their own academic progress.	The teacher gathers, analyzes, and uses data, including state assessment data, to measure learner progress, guide instruction, and provide timely feedback.	The teacher attempts to use a selection of assessment strategies to link assessment to learning outcomes, or uses assessment to plan/modify instruction, but is often ineffective.	The teacher consistently does not to use baseline or feedback data to make instructional decisions and does not report on learner progress in a timely manner.

Performance Standard 5: Learning Environment

Definition

The teacher provides a safe, student-centered environment that is academically challenging and respectful.

Sample Quality Indicators

The teacher

- ♦ promotes a climate of trust and teamwork within the classroom.
- ♦ respects and promotes the appreciation of diversity within the classroom.
- ♦ emphasizes continuous improvement toward student achievement.
- ♦ creates and maintains a physical setting that minimizes disruption and promotes learning and safety.

♦ establishes and maintains effective classroom rules and procedures communicating them to students and families.

♦ models caring, fairness, humor, courtesy, respect, active listening, and enthusiasm for learning.

♦ creates an attractive, warm, and supportive classroom environment.

Performance Appraisal Rubrics

Three-Point Performance Rubric for Learning Environment

Proficient*	Needs Improvement	Unsatisfactory
The teacher uses resources, routines, and procedures to provide a positive, safe, student-centered environment that is academically challenging and respectful.	The teacher inconsistently demonstrates expectations for student behavior and/or achievement.	The teacher rarely maintains acceptable expectations for student behavior and/or academic achievement.

* "Proficient" is the baseline of acceptable performance for teachers and is the actual performance standard.

Four-Point Performance Rubric for Learning Environment

Exemplary *In addition to meeting the standard…*	Proficient*	Needs Improvement	Unsatisfactory
The teacher consistently uses effective management strategies so that learning time is maximized and disruptions are minimized.	The teacher provides a well-managed, safe, student-centered environment that is academically challenging and respectful.	The teacher inconsistently addresses student behavior and needs required for a safe, positive social and academic environment.	The teacher inadequately addresses student behavior, displays a poor attitude with students, and/or ignores safety standards.

* "Proficient" is the baseline of acceptable performance for teachers and is the actual performance standard.

Five-Point Performance Rubric for Learning Environment

Exemplary *The professional's work is exceptional. In addition to meeting the standard…*	Superior *In addition to meeting the standard…*	Proficient *The description is the actual performance standard.*	Developing/ Needs Improvement	Unsatisfactory
The teacher consistently provides a well-managed, safe, student-centered environment that is academically challenging and respectful.	The teacher often uses effective management strategies so that learning time is maximized and disruptions are minimized.	The teacher creates and maintains a safe classroom environment while encouraging fairness, respect, and enthusiasm.	The teacher attempts to address student behavior and needs required for a safe, positive, social, and academic environment, but is often ineffective.	The teacher consistently addresses student behavior in an ineffective manner or does not maintain a safe, equitable learning environment.

Performance Standard 6: Communication and Advocacy

Definition

The teacher communicates effectively with students, school personnel, families, and the community to enhance, promote, and advocate for student learning

Sample Quality Indicators

The teacher

♦ uses precise language, correct vocabulary and grammar, and acceptable forms of oral and written expression.

♦ explains directions, concepts and lesson content to students in a logical, sequential, and age-appropriate manner.

♦ shares major instructional goals and classroom expectations with families.

♦ initiates communication and responds to families or guardians concerning student expectations, progress or problems in a timely and confidential manner.

♦ coordinates efforts with school staff, other service providers, and community resources to reach educational decisions that enhance student learning.

- demonstrates sensitivity to the social and cultural background of students, parent and others.

- models various effective communication strategies.

- adheres to school and district policies regarding communication of student information.

- collaborates with colleagues from other fields/content areas in the integration of instruction and/or services.

- supports, promotes, and communicates the mission, vision, and goals of the school and school district.

Performance Appraisal Rubrics

Three-Point Performance Rubric for Communication and Advocacy

Proficient*	Needs Improvement	Unsatisfactory
The teacher communicates effectively with students, school personnel, families, and the community to enhance, promote, and advocate for student learning.	The teacher inconsistently communicates with students, staff, parents, or community in an effective manner and/or inconsistently communicates concepts and class expectations to students.	The teacher rarely communicates and responds to students, staff, parents, or community concerns and/or poorly articulates content and expectations to students.

* "Proficient" is the baseline of acceptable performance for teachers and is the actual performance standard.

Four-Point Performance Rubric for Communication and Advocacy

Exemplary *In addition to meeting the standard…*	Proficient*	Needs Improvement	Unsatisfactory
The teacher uses a variety of communication techniques to inform, network, and collaborate with others to enhance student learning.	The teacher communicates effectively with students, school personnel, families, and the community.	The teacher inconsistently or ineffectively communicates with others.	The teacher inadequately communicates with school community by poorly acknowledging concerns, responding to inquiries, and/or encouraging involvement with stakeholders.

* "Proficient" is the baseline of acceptable performance for teachers and is the actual performance standard.

Five-Point Performance Rubric for Communication and Advocacy

Exemplary	Superior	Proficient	Developing/ Needs Improvement	Unsatisfactory
The professional's work is exceptional. In addition to meeting the standard…	*In addition to meeting the standard…*	*The description is the actual performance standard.*		
The teacher consistently uses a variety of communication techniques to inform, network, and collaborate with students, staff, and other members of the learning community to enhance student learning.	The teacher often communicates information and responds to students and other stakeholders in a highly effective manner.	The teacher communicates effectively with students, their parents or families, staff, and other members of the learning community.	The teacher often communicates with students, staff, and other members of the learning community in an inconsistent or ineffective manner.	The teacher consistently does not communicate effectively with students, staff and other members of the learning community.

Performance Standard 7: Professionalism

Definition

The teacher maintains a professional demeanor, participates in professional growth opportunities, and contributes to the profession.

Sample Quality Indicators

The teacher

- ◆ maintains a professional demeanor and behavior (e.g., appearance, punctuality, attendance).

- ◆ respects and maintains confidentiality and assumes responsibility for professional actions.

- ◆ handles administrative routines, policies, and procedures quickly and efficiently.

- ◆ represents the school/community favorably.

♦ evaluates and identifies areas of personal strength and weakness related to professional skills and their impact on student learning and sets goals for improvement of skills and professional performance.

♦ participates in professional growth activities (e.g., mentoring, peer coaching, and/or supervising practicing teachers or interns, attending conferences, participating in workshops, pursuing course work, and/or belonging to professional organizations at the district, state, and/or national level).

♦ serves on school and/or district committees and supports school activities.

Performance Appraisal Rubrics

Three-Point Performance Rubric for Professionalism

Proficient*	Needs Improvement	Unsatisfactory
The teacher maintains a commitment to professional ethics and the mission of the school. The teacher takes responsibility for and participates in professional growth that results in enhancement of student learning.	The teacher inconsistently demonstrates professional judgment, supports the school's mission, participates in professional growth activities, or applies strategies and information from professional growth opportunities.	The teacher demonstrates poor professional judgment, fails to support the school's mission, rarely takes advantage of professional growth opportunities, or fails to fulfill professional responsibilities.

* "Proficient" is the baseline of acceptable performance for teachers and is the actual performance standard.

Four-Point Performance Rubric for Professionalism

Exemplary *In addition to meeting the standard…*	Proficient*	Needs Improvement	Unsatisfactory
The teacher is a professional role model for others, engages in a high level of personal professional growth, and contributes to the development of others and the well-being of the profession.	The teacher maintains a professional demeanor, participates in professional growth opportunities, and contributes to the profession.	The teacher inconsistently participates in professional growth activities, and opportunities to serve the profession, and/or displays lapses in professional judgment.	The teacher demonstrates inflexibility, a reluctance to support others in the work of the school, and rarely takes advantage of professional growth opportunities.

* "Proficient" is the baseline of acceptable performance for teachers and is the actual performance standard.

Five-Point Performance Rubric for Professionalism

Exemplary	Superior	Proficient	Developing/ Needs Improvement	Unsatisfactory
The professional's work is exceptional. In addition to meeting the standard…	*In additional to meeting the standard…*	*The description is the actual performance standard.*		
The teacher at a high level consistently demonstrates professional conduct, contributes to the professional growth of others, and assumes a leadership role within the learning community.	The teacher demonstrates a high level of professional conduct, often engages in a high level of professional growth, and contributes to the professional development of others.	The teacher demonstrates behavior consistent with legal, ethical, and professional standards and engages in continuous professional growth.	The teacher often does not display professional judgment or only occasionally participates in professional development activities.	The teacher does not adhere to legal, ethical, or professional standards, including all requirements for professional development activities.

Performance Standard 8: Student Progress

Definition

The work of the teacher results in acceptable, measurable progress based on established standards.

Sample Quality Indicators

The teacher

- ◆ sets measurable and appropriate achievement goals for student progress.
- ◆ gathers and analyzes data on student academic achievement through standardized test results and other student performance sources.
- ◆ uses formative assessment to regularly monitor student progress and modify instruction as needed.
- ◆ provides evidence that achievement goals have been met.
- ◆ communicates/collaborates with colleagues in order to improve students' performance.

Performance Appraisal Rubrics

Three-Point Performance Rubric for Student Progress

Proficient*	Needs Improvement	Unsatisfactory
The work of the teacher results in acceptable, measurable student progress.	The work of the teacher inconsistently results in an acceptable level of student progress.	The work of the teacher rarely results in an acceptable level of student progress.

* "Proficient" is the baseline of acceptable performance for teachers and is the actual performance standard.

Four-Point Performance Rubric for Student Progress

Exemplary *In addition to meeting the standard…*	Proficient*	Needs Improvement	Unsatisfactory
The teacher attains a high level of student achievement with all populations of learners.	The work of the teacher results in acceptable, measurable progress based on established standards.	The work of the teacher results in student growth but does not meet the established standard and/or is not achieved with all populations taught by the teacher.	The work of the teacher does not achieve acceptable student growth.

* "Proficient" is the baseline of acceptable performance for teachers and is the actual performance standard.

Five-Point Performance Rubric for Student Progress

Exemplary *The professional's work is exceptional. In addition to meeting the standard…*	Superior *In addition to meeting the standard…*	Proficient *The description is the actual performance standard.*	Developing/ Needs Improvement	Unsatisfactory
The teacher consistently takes a key leadership role in assisting other professionals to achieve high levels of learner progress, or the work of the teacher consistently results in recognition of high levels of learner progress or achievement.	The work of the teacher often results in a high level of student achievement and/or progress.	The work of the teacher results in acceptable and measurable learner progress based on established standards, district goals, and/or school goals.	The work of the teacher results in some student progress, but more progress is often needed to meet established standards, district goals, and/or school goals.	The work of the teacher consistently does not result in acceptable student progress.

Informal Classroom Observation Form

Teacher Observed: _____ School: _____

Date: _____ Time: _____ Contract Status: ☐Pretenure ☐Tenure

1. KNOWLEDGE OF CURRICULUM, SUBJECT CONTENT, & DEVELOPMENTAL NEEDS • Appropriate curriculum standards • Key concepts are integrated • Higher-order thinking skills • Relationship to past/future • Accurate knowledge • High expectation • Knowledge of development	SPECIFIC EXAMPLES:
2. INSTRUCTIONAL PLANNING • Clear, logical, integrated plans • Content alignment • Coherent instructional plans • Curriculum materials • Differentiates instruction	SPECIFIC EXAMPLES:
3. INSTRUCTIONAL DELIVERY • Varied strategies • Variety of resources • Appropriate pacing • Student involvement • Relevance of instruction	SPECIFIC EXAMPLES:
4. ASSESSMENT OF LEARNING • Pre-/postassessment • Timely feedback • Teacher records • Student ownership • Reteaches/accelerates	SPECIFIC EXAMPLES:

5. LEARNING ENVIRONMENT • Climate of trust and respect • Diversity appreciation • Continuous improvement • Classroom rules/routines • Active listening, caring, fair • Safe and attractive area	SPECIFIC EXAMPLES:
6. COMMUNICATION • Correct language usage • Clear directions and explanations • Parent/family communication • Staff communication • Work relationships maintained	SPECIFIC EXAMPLES:
7. PROFESSIONALISM • Appearance and demeanor • Confidentiality is maintained • Professional growth activities • Contributions to the school • Contributions to the profession	SPECIFIC EXAMPLES:
8. STUDENT PROGRESS • Student achievement goals • Data collection • Formative assessment • Instructional modification • Evidence of goal attainment • Collaboration with others	SPECIFIC EXAMPLES:

Observer's Signature:_____

☐ White copy – Teacher ☐ Yellow copy – Principal

Formal Classroom Observation Form

Directions: This form is to be used with pretenure and tenured teachers. Observers will use the form to provide feedback to teachers about the observation. The yellow copy is given to the teacher and the white copy is for use by the observer/evaluator.

Teacher's Name _____   Date Observed _____   Time _____

The teacher is: ☐ Pretenured ☐ Tenured

Observer's Name _____

---

1. Knowledge of Curriculum, Subject Content, and Developmental Needs

The teacher demonstrates an understanding of the curriculum, subject content, and the developmental needs of students by providing relevant learning experiences.

- ◆ Appropriate curriculum standards
- ◆ Key concepts are integrated
- ◆ Higher-order thinking skills
- ◆ Relationship to past/future

- ◆ Accurate knowledge
- ◆ High expectation
- ◆ Knowledge of development

Comments

---

2. Instructional Planning

The teacher's planning uses appropriate curricula, instructional strategies, and resources to address the needs of all students.

- ◆ Clear, logical, integrated plans
- ◆ Content alignment
- ◆ Coherent instructional plans

- ◆ Curriculum materials
- ◆ Differentiates instruction

Comments

3. Instructional Delivery

The teacher promotes student learning by addressing individual learning differences and by using effective instructional strategies.

- ◆ Varied strategies
- ◆ Variety of resources
- ◆ Appropriate pacing

- ◆ Student involvement
- ◆ Relevance of instruction

Comments

4. Assessment of Learning

The teacher systematically gathers, analyzes, and uses data to measure student progress, guide instruction, and provide timely feedback.

- ◆ Pre-/postassessment
- ◆ Timely feedback
- ◆ Teacher records

- ◆ Student ownership
- ◆ Reteaches/accelerates

Comments

5. Learning Environment

The teacher provides a well-managed, safe, student-centered environment that is academically challenging and respectful.

- ◆ Climate of trust and respect
- ◆ Diversity appreciation
- ◆ Continuous improvement

- ◆ Classroom rules/routines
- ◆ Active listening, caring, fair
- ◆ Safe and attractive area

Comments

6. Communication and Advocacy

The teacher communicates effectively with students, school personnel, families, and the community.

- Correct language usage
- Clear directions and explanations
- Parent/family communication
- Staff communication
- Work relationships maintained

Comments

7. Professionalism

The teacher maintains a professional demeanor, participates in professional growth opportunities, and contributes to the profession.

- Appearance and demeanor
- Confidentiality is maintained
- Professional growth activities
- Contributions to the school
- Contributions to the profession

Comments

8. Student Progress

The work of the teacher results in acceptable, measurable progress based on established standards.

- Student achievement goals
- Data collection
- Formative assessment
- Instructional modification
- Evidence of goal attainment
- Collaboration with others

Comments

_____   _____
Observer's Signature/Date   Teacher's Signature/Date

Want to Know More?

Suggested Books by the Author Related to Teacher Effectiveness and Teacher Assessment

Stronge, J.H., & Grant, L.W. (2009, March). *Student achievement goal setting: Using data to improve teaching and learning.* **Larchmont, NY: Eye On Education.**

This book focus on improving student achievement through academic goal setting—a process in which teachers:

♦ Determine benchmark performance for the students;

♦ Set achievement goals based on where the students begin;

♦ Monitor progress throughout the academic year or other learning period; and finally,

♦ Measure performance at the end of the academic unit/year.

Student achievement goal setting provides a fair, realistic, and feasible method to implement instruction in order to increase student achievement in any school or classroom.

Stronge, J. H. (2007). *Qualities of effective teachers* **(2nd ed.). Alexandria, VA: Association for Supervision and Curriculum Development.**

This book provides researched-based and easy-to-use summaries and tools for teacher effectiveness. It identifies the common background factors and behaviors that characterize effectiveness in the classroom.

Stronge, J. H. (Ed.). (2006). *Evaluating teaching: A guide to current thinking and best practice* **(2nd ed.). Thousand Oaks, CA: Corwin Press.**

This volume, containing three major sections and thirteen chapters, synthesizes current research and thinking about teacher evaluation and blends research with practice. It provides a coherent and comprehensive guide for designing, implementing, and monitoring teacher evaluation system.

Stronge, J. H., Gareis, C. R., & Little, C. A. (2006). *Teacher pay and teacher quality: Attracting, developing, and retaining the best teachers.* **Thousand Oaks, CA: Corwin Press.**

This book illustrates the connection between the issue of teacher pay and the issues of teacher quality, student achievement, and school purposes. It also provides a sequential and practical approach for developing a comprehensive teacher compensation system based on research and best practices.

Stronge, J. H., & Hindman, J. L. (2006). *Teacher quality index: A protocol for teacher selection.* **Alexandria, VA: Association for Supervision and Curriculum Development.**

Based on the teacher quality indicators from *Qualities of Effective Teachers* (2nd ed., 2007), this book provides a research-based protocol help administrators select and hire teachers who will increase student achievement.

Stronge, J. H., & Grant, L. W. (2009). *Student achievement goal setting: Using data to improve teaching and learning.* **Larchmont, NY: Eye On Education.**

This book equips teachers and educational specialists with research-based tools and a plan of action so that they can use student achievement data to improve instructional practice and student academic performance.

Stronge, J. H., & Tucker, P. D. (2003). *Handbook on teacher evaluation.* **Larchmont, NY: Eye on Education.**

Easy-to-use and flexible tools have been developed to help administrators to implement teacher evaluation based on current thinking and best practices. The tools included in this book have been field tested in more than 500 schools.

Stronge, J. H., & Tucker, P. D. (2003). *Handbook on educational specialist evaluation.* **Larchmont, NY: Eye on Education.**

A framework is provided for designing a quality evaluation system for educational specialists. This book offer structured and logic procedures for designing performance standards, rating, and documenting performance of educational specialists.

Stronge, J. H., Tucker, P. D., & Hindman, J. L. (2004). *Handbook for qualities of effective teachers.* **Alexandria, VA: Association for Supervision and Curriculum Development. (Note: published in Chinese, 2006)**

This book provides an in-depth understanding of the qualities of teachers who yield student achievement progress. As a companion to *Qualities of Effective Teachers*, this book makes the qualities easier to implement within professional development or self-improvement program.

Tucker, P. D., & Stronge, J. H. (2005). *Linking teacher evaluation and student learning.* **Alexandria, VA: Association for Supervision and Curriculum Development.**

This book introduces evaluators to ways to incorporate student achievement in teacher assessment system. Organizers and rubrics are provided to enable practitioners to apply the book's methodologies in authentic situation.

References

Aaronson, D., Barrow, L., & Sander, W. (2007). Teachers and student achievement in the Chicago public high schools. *Journal of Labor Economics, 25*(1), 95–135.

Allington, R. L., & Johnston, P. H. (2000). *What do we know about effective fourth-grade teachers and their classrooms?* Albany, NY: The National Research Center on English Leaning & Achievement, State University of New York.

Au, W. (2007). High-stakes testing and curricular control: A qualitative metasynthesis. *Educational Researcher, 36*, 258–267.

Barney, D. (2005). Elementary physical education student teachers' interactions with students. *Physical Educator, 62*(3), 130–135.

Bembry, K. L., Jordan, H. R., Gomez, E., Anderson, M. C., & Mendro, R. L. (1998, April). *Policy implications of long-term teacher effects on student achievement.* Paper presented at the 1998 Annual Meeting of the American Educational Research Association, San Diego, CA.

Black, P. J., & Wiliam, D. (1998) Assessment and classroom learning. *Assessment in Education: Principles, Policy & Practice, 5*(1), 7–73.

Borko, H., & Elliott, R. (1999). Hands-on pedagogy versus hands-off accountability. *Phi Delta Kappan, 80*(5), 394–400.

Borko, H., & Livingston, C. (1989). Cognition and improvisation: Differences in mathematics instruction by expert and novice teachers. *American Educational Research Journal, 26*(4), 473–498.

Buttram, J. L., & Waters, J. T. (1997). Improving America's schools through standards-based education. *Bulletin, 81*(590), 1–5.

Cameron, C. E., Connor, C. M., Morrison, F. J., & Jewkes, A. M. (2008). Effects of classroom organization on letter-word reading in first grade. *Journal of School Psychology, 46*, 173–192.

Camphire, G. (2001). Are our teachers good enough? *SEDLetter, 13*(2). Retrieved November 12, 2001 from http://www.sedl.org/pubs/sedletter/v13n2/1.htm.

Carlson, E., Lee, H., & Schroll, K. (2004). Identifying attributes of high quality special education teachers. *Teacher Education and Special Education, 27*, 350–359.

Carter, P. J. (2003). *A review of highly effective teachers in Hamilton County: Analysis of current trends and implications for improvement.* Chattanooga, TN: Public Education Foundation. Retrieved November 7, 2008, from http://pef.ddngroup.com/.

Catt, S., Miller, D., & Schallenkamp, K. (2007). You are the key: Communicate for learning effectiveness. *Education, 127*(3), 369–377.

Cawelti, G. (1999). *Handbook of research on improving student achievement* (2nd ed.). Arlington, VA: Educational Research Service.

Cawelti, G. (Ed.). (2004). *Handbook of research on improving student achievement* (3rd ed.). Arlington, VA: Educational Research Service.

Chappius, S., & Stiggins, R. J. (2002). *Classroom assessment for learning. Educational Leadership, 60*(1), 40–43.

Cochran, K., DeRuiter, L., & King, R. (1993). Pedagogical content knowledge: An integrative model for teacher preparation. *Journal of Teacher Education, 4*, 18–29.

Cohen, D. K., Raudenbush, S. W., & Ball, D. L. (2003). Resources, instruction, and research. *Educational Evaluation and Policy Analysis, 25*(2), 119–142.

Collinson, V., Killeavy, M., & Stephenson, H. J. (1999). Exemplary teachers: Practicing an ethic of care in England, Ireland, and the United States. *Journal for a Just and Caring Education, 5*(4), 349–366.

Corbett, D., Wilson, B., & Williams, B. (2002). *Effort and excellence in urban classrooms: Expecting and getting success with all students.* New York, NY: Teachers College Press.

Cornett-DeVito, M., & Worley, D. W. (2005). A front row seat: A phenomenological investigation of students with learning disabilities. *Communication Education, 54,* 312–333.

Cotton, K. (2000). *The schooling practices that matter most.* Portland, OR: Northwest Regional Educational Laboratory.

Covino, E. A., & Iwanicki, E. (1996). Experienced teachers: Their constructs on effective teaching. *Journal of Personnel Evaluation in Education, 11,* 325–363.

Craig, J. & Cairo, L. (2005, December). *Assessing the relationship between questioning and understanding to improve learning and thinking (QUILT) and student achievement in mathematics: A pilot study.* Charleston, WV: Appalachia Educational Laboratory.

Cruickshank, D. R., & Haefele, D. (2001). Good teachers, plural. *Educational Leadership, 58*(5), 26–30.

Danielson, C. (2001). New Trends in teacher evaluation. *Educational Leadership, 58*(5), 12–15.

Danielson, C. (2002). *Enhancing student achievement: A framework for school improvement.* Alexandria, VA: Association for Supervision and Curriculum Development.

Darling-Hammond, L. (2001). The challenge of staffing our schools. *Educational Leadership, 58*(8), 12–17.

David, J. L. (2008). Pacing guides. *Educational Leadership, 66*(2), 87–88.

Dolezal, S. E., Welsh, L. M., Pressley, M., & Vincent, M. M. (2003). How third-grade teachers motivate student academic achievement. *The Elementary School Journal, 103,* 239–267.

Downey, C. J., Steffy, B. E., English, F. W., Frase, L. E., & Poston, W. K., Jr. (2004). *The three-minute classroom walk-through: Changing school supervisory practice on teacher at a time.* Thousand Oaks, CA: Corwin Press.

Dunn, R., Honigsfeld, A., Shea Doolan, L., Bostrom, L., Russo, K., Schiering, M.S., Suh, B. (2009). Impact of learning-style instructional strategies on students' achievement and attitudes: Perceptions of educators in diverse institutions. *Clearing House: A Journal of Educational Strategies, Issues, and Ideas, 82*(3), 135–140.

Education USA Special Report. (n.d.). *Good teachers: What to look for.* Arlington, VA: The National School Public Relations Association.

Educational Review Office. (1998). *The capable teacher.* Retrieved online on January 19, 2002, from http://www.ero.govt.nz/Publications/eers1998/98no2hl.html.

Emmer, E. T., & Stough, L. M. (2001). Classroom management: A critical part of educational psychology, with implications for teacher education. *Educational Psychologist, 36*(2), 103–112.

Emmer, E. T., Evertson, C. M., & Anderson, L. M. (1980). Effective classroom management at the beginning of the year. *The Elementary School Journal, 80*(5), 219–231.

Emmer, E. T., Evertson, C. M., & Worsham, M. E. (2003). *Classroom management for secondary teachers.* Boston: Allyn and Bacon.

Frase, L. E., & Streshly, W. (1994). Lack of accuracy, feedback, and commitment in teacher evaluation. *Journal of Personnel Evaluation in Education, 8*(1), 47–57.

Fraser, B. J., & Fisher, D. L. (1982). Predicting students' outcomes from their perceptions of classroom psycho-social environment. *American Educational Research Journal, 19,* 498–518.

Fuchs, L. S., Deno, S. L., & Mirkin, P. K. (1984). The effects of frequent curriculum-based measurement and evaluation on pedagogy, student achievement, and student awareness of learning. *American Educational Research Journal, 21*(2), 449–460.

Fullan, M. G. (1993). Why teachers must become change agents. *Educational Leadership, 50*(6), 12–17.

Goldhaber, D. D., & Brewer, D. J. (1997). Evaluating the effects of teacher degree level on educational performance. In W. J. Fowler (Ed.), *Developments in school finance, 1996* (pp. 197–210). Washington, DC: National Center for Educational Statistics, U.S. Department of Education.

Goldhaber, D. D., & Brewer, D. J. (2000). Does teacher certification matter? High school certification status and student achievement. *Educational Evaluation and Policy Analysis, 22*(2), 129–145.

Good, T. L., & Brophy, J. E. (1997). *Looking in classrooms* (7th ed.). New York, NY: Addison-Wesley.

Gronlund, N. E. (2006). *Assessment of student achievement* (8th ed.). Boston,, MA: Pearson.

Guskey, T. R. (2002). Does it make a difference? Evaluating professional development. *Educational Leadership, 59*(6), 45–51.

Guskey, T. R. (2007). Multiple sources of evidence: An analysis of stakeholders' perceptions of various indicators of student learning. *Educational Measurement: Issues and Practice, 26*(1), 19–27.

Hamilton, L., & Stecher, B. (2004). Responding effectively to test-based accountability. *Phi Delta Kappan, 85*(8), 578–583.

Hamre, B. K., & Pianta, R. C. (2005). Can instruction and emotional support in the first-grade classroom make a difference for children at risk of school failure? *Child Development, 76*(5), 949–967.

Hanushek, E. A., Kain, J. F., O'Brien, D. M., & Rivkin, S. G. (2005). *The market for teacher quality.* Cambridge, MA: National Bureau of Economic Research. Retrieved December 6, 2008, from http://www.nber.org/papers/w11154.pdf.

Hanushek, E. A., Kain, J. F., & Rivkin, S. G. (1998, August). *Teachers, schools, and academic achievement.* Cambridge, MA: National Bureau of Economic Research. Retrieved January 24, 2009, from http://www.nber.org/papers/w6691.

Harris, D. N., & Sass, T. R. (2007). *Teacher training, teacher quality and student achievement.* Washington, DC: National Center for Analysis of Longitudinal Data in Education Research. Retrieved April 4, 2009, from www.caldercenter.org/PDF/1001059_Teacher_Training.pdf.

Hattie, J. (2003). *Teachers make a difference: What is the research evidence?* Retrieved December 12, 2008, from http://www.leadspace.govt.nz/leadership/pdf/john_hattie.pdf.

Haynie, G. (2006, April). *Effective Biology teaching: A value-added instructional improvement analysis model.* Retrieved February 7, 2009, from http://www.wcpss.net/evaluation-research/reports/2006/0528biology.pdf.

Heneman, H. G., & Milanowski, A. T. (2003). Continuing assessment of teacher reactions to a standards-based teacher evaluation system. *Journal of Personnel Evaluation in Education, 17*(2), 173–195.

Hershberg, T. (2005). Value-added assessment and systemic reform: A response to the challenge of human capital development. *Phi Delta Kappan, 87*(4), 276–283.

Hess, F. M. (2008, December/2009, January). The new stupid. *Educational Leadership, 66*(4), 12–17.

Hiebert, J., Gallimore, R., & Stigler, J. W. (2003, November 5). The new heroes of teaching. *Education Week, 23*(10). Retrieved November 10, 2003, from www.edweek.com/ew/ewstory.cfm?slug=10hiebert.h23.

Hill, H. C., Rowan, B., & Ball, D. L. (2005). Effects of teachers' mathematical knowledge for teaching on student achievement. *American Educational Research Journal, 42*, 371–406.

ISTE Research Reports. (n.d.). Overview: Research on IT [informational technology] in education. Accessed on September 22, 2002 from http://www.iste.org/research/reports /tlcu/overview.html.

Johnson, B. L. (1997). An organizational analysis of multiple perspectives of effective teaching: Implications for teacher evaluation. *Journal of Personnel Evaluation in Education, 11,* 69–87.

Johnston, D. L. (1999). The seven no-no's of performance evaluation. *School Administrator, 56*(11), 361–381.

Jones, B. D., & Egley, R. J. (2004). Voice from the frontlines: Teachers' perceptions of high-stakes testing. *Educational Policy Analysis Archives, 12*(39). Retrieved November 17, 2007, from http://epaa.asu.edu/epaa/va12n39.

Jones, G., Jones, B. D., Hardin, B., Chapman, L., Yardrough, T., & Davis, M. (1999). The impact of high-stakes testing on teachers and students in North Carolina. *Phi Delta Kappan, 81*(3), 199–203.

Keller, B. (2008, January 16). Drive on to improve evaluation systems for teachers. *Education Week, 27(19),* 8.

Kunter, M., Baumert, J., & Koller, P. (2007). Effective classroom management and the development of subject-related interest. *Learning and Instruction, 17,* 494–509.

Kunter, M., Tsiam Y., Klusmann, U., Brunner, M., Krauss, S., & Baumert, J. (2008). Students' and mathematics teachers' perceptions of teacher enthusiasm and instruction. *Learning and Instruction, 18,* 468–482.

Leinhardt, G. (1993). On teaching. In R. Glaser (Ed.), *Advances in instructional psychology,* Vol. 4 (pp. 1–54). Hillsdale, NJ: Lawrence Erlbaum Associates.

Little, J. W. (1993). Teachers' professional development in a climate of educational reform. *Educational Evaluation and Policy Analysis, 15*(2), 129–151.

Long, J. F., & Hoy, A. W. (2005). Interested instructors: A composite portrait of individual differences and effectiveness. *Teaching and Teacher Education, 22*(3), 303–314.

Loup, K. S., Garland, J. S., Ellett, C. D., & Rugutt, J. K. (1996). Ten years later: Findings from a republication of a study of teacher evaluation practices in our 100 largest school districts. *Journal of Personnel Evaluation in Education, 10*(3), 203–226.

Lovelace, M.K. (2005). Meta-analysis of experimental research based on the Dunn and Dunn model. *Journal of Educational Research, 98*(3), 176–183.

Ludtke, O., Robitzsch, A., Trautwein, U., & Kunter, M. (2009). Assessing the impact of learning environments: How to use student ratings of classroom or school characteristics in multilevel modeling. *Contemporary Educational Psychology, 34,* 120–131.

Lumpkin, A. (2007). Caring teachers: The key to student learning. *Kappa Delta Pi Record, 43*(4), 158–160.

Marzano, R. J., Marzano, R. J., & Pickering, D. J. (2003). *Classroom management that works: Research-based strategies for every teacher.* Alexandria, VA: Association for Supervision and Curriculum Development.

Marzano, R. J., Pickering, D., & McTighe, J. (1993). *Assessing student outcomes: Performance assessment using the dimensions of learning model.* Alexandria, VA: Association for Supervision and Curriculum Development.

McDonald, F. J., & Elias, P. (1976). Executive summary report: Beginning teacher evaluation study, phase II (PR-76–18). Princeton, NJ: Educational Testing Service.

McEwan, E. K. (2002). *10 Traits of highly effective teachers: How to hire, coach, and mentor successful teachers.* Thousand Oaks, CA: Corwin Press.

McKechnie, J. L. (Ed.). (1983). *Webster's new twentieth century dictionary* (2nd ed.). New York: Simon & Schuster.

Mendro, R. L., Jordan, H. R., Gomez, E., Anderson, M. C., & Bembry, K. L. (1998, April). *Longitudinal teacher effects on student achievement and their relation to school and project evaluation.*

Paper presented at the 1998 Annual Meeting of the American Educational Research Association, San Diego, CA.

Merriam-Webster, Inc. (2006). *Webster's new explorer encyclopedic dictionary.* Springfield, MA: Author.

Monk, D. H. (1994). Subject area preparation of secondary mathematics and science teachers and student achievement. *Economics of Education Review, 13*(2), 125–145.

Munoz, M. A., & Chang, F. C. (2007). The elusive relationship between teacher characteristics and student academic growth: A longitudinal multilevel model for change. *Journal of Personnel Evaluation in Education, 20*, 147–164.

National Association of Secondary School Principals (NASSP). (1997). Students say: What makes a good teacher? *Schools in the Middle, 6*(5), 15–17.

Nye, B., Konstantopoulos, S., & Hedges, L. V. (2004). How large are teacher effects? *Educational Evaluation and Policy Analysis, 26*(3), 237–257.

Palardy, G. J., & Rumberger, R. W. (2008). Teacher effectiveness in first grade: The importance of background qualifications, attitudes, and instructional practices for student learning. *Educational Evaluation and Policy Analysis, 30*(2), 111–140.

Panasuk, R., Stone, W., & Todd, J. (2002). Lesson planning strategy for effective mathematics teaching. *Education, 22*(2), 808–827.

Peart, N. A. & Campbell, F. A. (1999). At-risk students' perceptions of teacher effectiveness. *Journal for a Just and Caring Education, 5*(3), 269–284.

Peters, S., & Reid, D. K. (2009). Resistance and discursive practice: Promoting advocacy in teacher undergraduate and graduate programmes. *Teaching and Teacher Education, 25*(4), 551–558.

Pressley, M., Rapael, L. Gallagher, J. D., & DiBella, J. (2004). Providence-St. Mel School: How a school that works for African Americans works. *Journal of Educational Psychology, 96*(2), 216–235.

Rice, J. K. (2003). *Teacher quality: Understanding the effectiveness of teacher attributes.* Washington, DC: Economic Policy Institute.

Rivkin, S. G., Hanushek, E. A., & Kain, J. F. (2005). Teachers, schools, and academic achievement. *Econometrica, 73*(2), 417–458.

Rockoff, J. E. (2004). The impact of individual teachers on student achievement: Evidence from panel data. *The American Economic Review, 94*(2), 247–252.

Rockwell, R .E., Andre, L. C., & Hawley, M. K. (1996). *Parents and teachers as partners: Issues and challenges.* Fort Worth, TX: Harcourt Brace College.

Rowan, B., Chiang, F. S., & Miller, R. J. (1997). Using research on employees' performance to study the effects of teachers on student achievement. *Sociology of Education, 70*, 256–284.

Rowan, B., Correnti, R., & Miller, R. J. (2002). What large-scale, survey research tells us about teacher effects on student achievement: Insights from the *Prospects* study of elementary schools. *Teachers College Record, 104*(8), 1525–1567.

Rowan, B., Schilling, S. G., Ball, D. L., & Miller, R. (2001, October). *Measuring teachers' pedagogical content knowledge in surveys: An exploratory study.* Retrieved April 15, 2009, from http://www.sii.soe.umich.edu/documents/pck%20final%20report%20revised%20BR100901.pdf.

Sachs, J. (2001). Teacher professional identity: Competing discourse, competing outcomes. *Journal of Education Policy, 16*(2), 149–161.

Safer, N., & Fleischman, S. (2005). How student progress monitoring improves instruction. *Educational Leadership, 62*(5), 81–83.

Sanders, W. L., & Rivers, J. C. (1996, November). *Cumulative and residual effects of teachers on future student academic achievement.* Knoxville, TN: University of Tennessee Value-Added Research and Assessment Center.

Schacter, J., & Thum, Y. M. (2004). Paying for high- and low-quality teaching. *Economics of Education Review, 23*, 411–430.

Schalock, H. D., & Schalock, M. D. (1993). Student learning in teacher evaluation and school improvement: An introduction. *Journal of Personnel Evaluation in Education, 7*, 103–104.

Schalock, H. D., Schalock, M. D., Cowart, B., & Myton, D. (1993). Extending teacher assessment beyond knowledge and skills: An emerging focus on teacher accomplishments. *Journal of Personnel Evaluation in Education, 7*, 105–133.

School Board News. (1997). Teacher quality is key to student achievement (electronic version). *American School Board Journal.* Retrieved online November 21, 2000 from http://www.asbj.com/achievement/ci/ci3.html.

Schroeder, C.M., Scott, T. P., Tolson, H., Huang, T., & Lee, Y. (2007). A meta-analysis of national research: Effects of teaching strategies on student achievement in science in the United States. *Journal of Research in Science Teaching, 44*, 1436–1460.

Schulman, L. S. (1987). Knowledge and teaching: Foundations of the new reform. *Harvard Educational Review, 57*(1), 1–22.

Shellard, E., & Protheroe, N. (2000). Effective teaching: How do we know it when we see it? *The Informed Educator Series.* Arlington, VA: Educational Research Service.

Shepard, L. A., & Dougherty, K. C. (1991). *Effects of high-stakes testing on instruction.* Paper presented at the annual meeting of the American Educational Research Association and National Council on Measurement in Education, Chicago, IL.

Stecher, B. M., & Mitchell, K. J. (1995). *Portfolio driven reform: Vermont teachers' understanding of mathematical problem solving. CSE technical report 400.* Los Angeles, CA: National Center for Research on Evaluation, Standards, and Student Testing.

Stecker, P. M., Fuchs, L. S., & Fuchs, D. (2005). Using curriculum-based measurement to improve student achievement: Review of research. *Psychology in the Schools, 42*(8), 795–819.

Stiggins, R. J. (1999). Assessment, student confidence, and school success. *Phi Delta Kappan, 81*(3), 191–199.

Stiggins, R. J. (2002). Assessment crisis: The absence of assessment for learning. *Phi Delta Kappan, 83*(10), 758–764.

Stiggins, R., & DuFour, R. (2009). Maximizing the power of formative assessments. *Phi Delta Kappan, 90*(9), 640–644.

Strauss, R. P., & Sawyer, E. A. (1986). Some new evidence on teacher and student competencies. *Economics of Education Review, 5*, 41–48.

Stronge, J. H. (Ed). (2006). *Evaluating teaching: A guide to current thinking and best practice* (2nd ed.). Thousand Oaks, CA: Corwin Press.

Stronge, J. H. (2007). *Qualities of effective teachers* (2nd ed.). Alexandria, VA: Association of Supervision and Curriculum Development.

Stronge, J. H., Little, C., & Grant, L. W. (2008, July 16). *Gifted teachers for gifted students: An international comparative study of national award-winning teachers.* Paper presented at the Asia-Pacific Conference on Gifted, Singapore.

Stronge, J. H., & Tucker, P. D. (2003a). *Handbook on teacher evaluation.* Larchmont, NY: Eye On Education.

Stronge, J. H., & Tucker, P. D. (2003b). *Handbook on educational specialist evaluation.* Larchmont, NY: Eye On Education.

Stronge, J. H., Ward, T. J., Tucker, P. D., & Hindman, J. L. (2008). What is the relationship between teacher quality and student achievement? An exploratory study. *Journal of Personnel Evaluation in Education, 20*(3–4), 165–184.

Swap, S. A. (1993). *Developing home-school partnerships from concepts to practice.* New York, NY: Teachers College Press.

Thayer, Y. (2000). Virginia's Standards make all students stars. *Phi Delta Kappan, 57*(7), 70–72.

The role of teacher professionalism in education. (n.d.). Retrieved June 1, 2009, from http://students. ed.uiuc.edu/vallicel/Teacher_Professionalism.html.

Tobin, K. (1980). The effect of extended teacher wait-time on science achievement. *Journal of Research in Science Teaching, 17,* 469–475.

Tomlinson, C. A. (1999). *The differentiated classroom: Responding to the needs of all learners.* Alexandria, VA: Association for Supervision and Curriculum Development.

Tomlinson, C. A. (2001). *How to differentiate instruction in mixed-ability classrooms* (2nd ed.). Alexandria, VA: Association for Supervision and Curriculum Development.

Tomlinson, C.A. (2007). Learning to love assessment. *Educational Leadership, 65*(4), 8–13.

Tucker, P. D., & Stronge, J. H. (2003). *Handbook for teacher evaluation.* Larchmont, NY: Eye On Education.

Tucker, P. D., Stronge, J. H., & Gareis, C. R. (2002). *Handbook on teacher portfolios for evaluation and professional development.* Larchmont, NY: Eye On Education.

Vartuli, S. (2005). Beliefs: The heart of teaching. *Young Children, 60,* 76–86.

Vogler, K. E. (2002). The impact of high-stakes, state-mandated student performance assessment on teachers' instructional practices. *Education, 123*(1), 39–56.

Walberg, H. J. (1984). Improving the productivity of America's schools. *Educational Leadership, 41*(8), 19–27.

Walker, M. H. (1998). 3 Basics for better student output. *Education Digest, 63*(9), 15–18.

Walls, R. T., Nardi, A. H., von Minden, A. M., & Hoffman, N. (2002). The characteristics of effective and ineffective teachers. *Teacher education quarterly, 29*(1), 39–48.

Walsh, J. A., & Sattes, B. D. (2005). *Quality questioning: Research-based practice to engage every learner.* Thousand Oaks, CA: Corwin Press.

Wang, M. C., Haertel, G. D., & Walberg, H. J. (1994). What helps students learn? *Educational Leadership, 51*(4), 74–79.

Weiss, I. R., & Miller, B. (2006, October). *Deepening teacher content knowledge for teaching: A review of the evidence.* Retrieved May 10, 2009, from http://hub.mspnet.org/media/data/Weiss-Miller.pdf?media_000000002247.pdf.

Wenglisky, H. (2000). *How teaching matters: Bringing the classroom back into discussion of teacher quality.* Princeton, NJ: Millikan Family Foundation and Educational Testing Service.

Wenglinsky, H. (2002). How schools matter: The link between teacher classroom practices and student academic performance. *Education Policy Analysis Archives, 10*(12). Retrieved November 20, 2008, from http://epaa.asu.edu/epaa/v10n12/.

Wenglinsky, H. (2004). The link between instructional practice and the racial gap in middle schools. *Research in Middle Level Education Online, 28*(1), 1–13.

Wolf, K., Lichtenstein, G., & Stevenson, C. (1997). Portfolios in teacher evaluation. In J. H. Stronge (Ed.), *Evaluating teaching: A guide to current thinking and best practice* (pp. 193–214). Thousand Oaks, CA: Corwin Press.

Worley, D., Tistworth, S., Worley, D. W., & Cornett-DeVito, M. (2007). Instructional communication competence: Lessons learned from award-winning teachers. *Communication Studies, 58*(2), 207–222.

Wright, S. P., Horn, S. P., & Sanders, W. L. (1997). Teacher and classroom context effects on student achievement: Implications for teacher evaluation. *Journal of Personnel Evaluation in Education, 11,* 57–67.

Yoon, K. S., Duncan, T., Lee, S. W., Scarloss, B., & Shapley, K. L. (2007, December). *Reviewing the evidence on how teacher professional development affects student achievement.* Washington, DC: Regional Educational Laboratory Southwest.

Zacharias, N. T. (2007). Teacher and student attitudes toward teacher feedback. *RELC Journal: A Journal of Language Teaching and Research, 38*(1), 38–52.

Zahorik, J., Halbach, A., Ehrle, K., & Molnar, A. (2003). Teaching practices for smaller classes. *Educational Leadership, 61*(1), 75–77.